MW00654408

This excellent book sets out a thoughtful, evi

guide for teachers and leaders alike. It provides practical support in conjunction with challenge and leadership, and it gives the reader a real sense of confidence in putting ideas into practice. Dr. Lang-Raad has artfully connected international standards, academic research, educational leadership, practical classroom application and structured activities, alongside so much more! As a result, the ideas contained within the book bring contemporary priorities to life and interweave them with established professional knowledge—saving the reader time, as well as ensuring robust, forward-facing, and very accessible advice. Another brilliant book from the fantastic Dr. Nathan Lang-Raad.

—Fiona Aubrey-Smith
founder, PedTech

AI isn't here to replace teachers—it's here to enhance what we do best. Dr. Lang-Raad's innovative HAIL model offers a friendly framework for thoughtfully integrating AI in the classroom. As an innovative teacher, I appreciate how this book provides realistic strategies to personalize learning while keeping human connections at the center of all we do.

—Tony Vincent
educator and AI consultant

Dr. Lang-Raad's new book is an extremely practical and valuable contribution to our usage of AI and other digital learning tools in P–12 education. Although written as a primer about effective AI integration in classrooms, *The AI Assist* includes numerous helpful reminders and strategies about other learning technologies as well. The HAIL framework is reinforced with multiple examples, templates, and checklists across grade levels and subject areas. The entire book is grounded in a deep understanding of educators' day-to-day work, which makes it immediately useful and actionable.

—Scott McLeod
professor of educational leadership
founding director, CASTLE, University of Colorado Denver

Dr. Lang-Raad presents a clear and practical guide for implementing current AI technologies into education. His strategies aim to enhance human capabilities and drive deeper learning outcomes for students. With a focus on safety and impactful pedagogical practices, readers of all skill levels will find this book immediately useful in the complex age of AI.

—David Hotler
educator and community builder

Dr. Lang-Raad does a masterful job of assuring classroom teachers of their irreplaceable role in education while offering a road map to engaging instruction that embraces artificial intelligence in the classroom. *The AI Assist* allows teachers to take a deep breath and lean confidently into the AI frontier.

—Vonda Dahl
literacy coordinator, Mandan Public Schools, North Dakota

THE
AI
ASSIST

Many ASCD members received this book
as a member benefit upon its initial release.
Learn more at www.ascd.org/memberbooks

THE AI ASSIST

Strategies for Integrating AI into the *Very Human* Act of Teaching

NATHAN LANG-RAAD

Arlington, Virginia USA

Arlington, Virginia USA

2800 Shirlington Rd., Suite 1001 • Arlington, VA 22206 USA
Phone: 800-933-2723 or 703-578-9600 • Fax: 703-575-5400
Website: www.ascd.org • Email: member@ascd.org
Author guidelines: www.ascd.org/write

ISTE®

2111 Wilson Boulevard, Suite 300 • Arlington, VA 22201 USA
Website: www.iste.org
ISTE® is a registered trademark of the International Society for Technology in Education.

Richard Culatta, *Chief Executive Director;* Anthony Rebora, *Chief Content Officer;* Genny Ostertag, *Managing Director, Book Acquisitions and Editing;* Bill Varner, *Senior Acquisitions Editor;* Mary Beth Nielsen, *Director, Book Editing;* Jamie Greene, *Senior Editor;* Beth Schlenoff, *Graphic Designer;* Circle Graphics, *Typesetter;* Kelly Marshall, *Production Manager;* Christopher Logan, *Senior Production Specialist;* Kathryn Oliver, *Creative Project Manager;* Shajuan Martin, *E-Publishing Specialist*

Copyright © 2025 ASCD. All rights reserved. It is illegal to reproduce copies of this work in print or electronic format (including reproductions displayed on a secure intranet or stored in a retrieval system or other electronic storage device from which copies can be made or displayed) without the prior written permission of the publisher. By purchasing only authorized electronic or print editions and not participating in or encouraging piracy of copyrighted materials, you support the rights of authors and publishers. Readers who wish to reproduce or republish excerpts of this work in print or electronic format may do so for a small fee by contacting the Copyright Clearance Center (CCC), 222 Rosewood Dr., Danvers, MA 01923, USA (phone: 978-750-8400; fax: 978-646-8600; web: www.copyright.com). To inquire about site licensing options or any other reuse, contact ASCD Permissions at www.ascd.org/permissions or permissions@ascd.org. For a list of vendors authorized to license ASCD ebooks to institutions, see www.ascd.org/epubs. Send translation inquiries to translations@ascd.org.

ASCD® is a registered trademark of Association for Supervision and Curriculum Development. All other trademarks contained in this book are the property of, and reserved by, their respective owners, and are used for editorial and informational purposes only. No such use should be construed to imply sponsorship or endorsement of the book by the respective owners.

All web links in this book are correct as of the publication date below but may have become inactive or otherwise modified since that time. If you notice a deactivated or changed link, please email books@ascd.org with the words "Link Update" in the subject line. In your message, please specify the web link, the book title, and the page number on which the link appears.

PAPERBACK ISBN: 978-1-4166-3333-4 ASCD product #124030
PDF EBOOK ISBN: 978-1-4166-3334-1; see Books in Print for other formats.
Quantity discounts are available: email programteam@ascd.org or call 800-933-2723, ext. 5773, or 703-575-5773.
For desk copies, go to www.ascd.org/deskcopy.

ASCD Member Book No. FY24-8 (Nov 2024 PSI+). ASCD Member Books mail to Premium (P), Select (S), and Institutional Plus (I+) members on this schedule: Jan, PSI+; Feb, P; Apr, PSI+; May, P; Jul, PSI+; Aug, P; Sep, PSI+; Nov, PSI+; Dec, P. For current details on membership, see www.ascd.org/membership.

Library of Congress Cataloging-in-Publication Data

Names: Lang-Raad, Nathan D., 1982- author.
Title: The AI assist : strategies for integrating AI into the very human act of teaching / Nathan Lang-Raad.
Other titles: Artificial intelligence assist
Description: Arlington, Virginia : ASCD : ISTE 2025. | Includes bibliographical references and index.
Identifiers: LCCN 2024035709 (print) | LCCN 2024035710 (ebook) | ISBN 9781416633334 (paperback) | ISBN 9781416633341 (adobe pdf) | ISBN 9781416633358 (epub)
Subjects: LCSH: Artificial intelligence—Educational applications. | Educational planning.
Classification: LCC LB1028.43 .L366 2025 (print) | LCC LB1028.43 (ebook) | DDC 371.33/463—dc23/eng/20240909
LC record available at https://lccn.loc.gov/2024035709
LC ebook record available at https://lccn.loc.gov/2024035710

31 30 29 28 27 26 25 1 2 3 4 5 6 7 8 9 10 11 12

THE AI ASSIST

Introduction: Embracing the Future of Education with AI

In 2022, AI became increasingly prevalent across society, from everyday applications to complex systems. While AI's potential made headlines in many sectors, its integration into education presented unique challenges. Unlike other industries where AI adoption was more straightforward, the landscape lacked clear guidelines for implementing these powerful tools in classrooms. Even now, the role of AI in education continues to evolve, leaving many educators without a clear road map.

This book aims to provide that essential guidance. It's crucial to remember that although AI offers significant opportunities to enhance learning, it should complement, not replace, the irreplaceable human qualities that define effective teaching. Empathy, creativity, and the ability to inspire students remain uniquely human traits. As educators, your role is to leverage AI in ways that support these human elements, ensuring technology enhances rather than diminishes the personal connections fundamental to education.

The integration of AI into education is inevitable; the questions now are when and how. This book serves as your strategic guide for effectively integrating AI into education, rather than simply reacting to technological change. It's important to understand AI's twofold impact: it may challenge conventional teaching approaches, but it also presents opportunities to amplify your role as an educator. AI can facilitate personalized learning experiences, allowing you to focus more on nurturing curiosity and building meaningful connections with your students.

As Ethan Mollick (2024) highlights, discussions about AI often fall into a false dichotomy—either AI is all "hype," or the age of superhuman machines is imminent. The reality lies somewhere in between. Current AI technologies, especially large language models (LLMs) like ChatGPT, Copilot, Claude, and DALL-E, are already proving to be valuable co-intelligence tools, significantly enhancing human performance in various tasks. These tools have shown their strengths in areas such as innovation, productivity, and coding, but we are still exploring their full potential.

The first wave of AI adoption was focused on individual use and saw some of the fastest adoption rates in history for a new technology. The second wave, however, involves integrating AI into organizational structures, which will be crucial for achieving true productivity growth. This integration is not just about efficiency or cost cutting; it's about understanding how AI can unlock new opportunities and drive innovation in education.

With each new wave of technology, including personal computers, the internet, and now generative AI, we must decide how to integrate these advancements into our learning environments. This is especially true for generative AI technologies like ChatGPT and DALL-E, which can profoundly support project-based, interest-driven creative learning experiences. By intentionally designing and using these tools, we can align AI integration with our educational values and visions, fostering environments in which students develop as creative, curious, collaborative learners.

This book aims to simplify AI for educators with a clear, practical guide. It is organized as a step-by-step journey, starting with the basics of AI and moving to hands-on classroom applications. Each chapter builds on the previous one, providing a logical and comprehensive progression through the topic. As we integrate AI into education, it is vital to ensure that these technologies support and enhance learner agency rather than constrain it. AI should provide students with opportunities to set their own goals, build on their interests, and feel a sense of ownership over their learning. Furthermore, we must recognize the value of human connection in teaching, ensuring that AI tools serve as supplements to, not replacements for, human teachers. This approach will help maintain a balance where AI enriches human interaction, creativity, and empathy in the classroom.

In this book, you will learn how to use large language models like ChatGPT for generating personalized writing prompts and providing instant feedback on student essays. You'll explore tools like DALL-E for creating unique and engaging visual aids that can bring complex concepts to life, making lessons more vivid and memorable. Additionally, we'll discuss Copilot as a real-time coding assistant that helps students with programming assignments by offering instant suggestions and debugging tips.

Throughout the chapters, these tools will be explicitly referenced, with clear pointers to the figures where you will find detailed descriptions and instructions for their effective use. Whether it's leveraging ChatGPT to enhance classroom discussions, using DALL-E to stimulate creativity through visual projects, or integrating Copilot to support computer science education, each tool is presented with practical applications and tips for maximizing their potential. This ensures that you have the resources and knowledge to seamlessly incorporate these advanced AI technologies into your teaching practice, thereby enriching the learning experience for your students.

Engage with this book as a dialogue. It is designed to be interactive, prompting you to reflect, challenge your current practices, and grow as an educator at the forefront of technological advancements in education. The narrative here is direct and practical, offering you deep insights and an understanding of how to apply AI effectively.

This new terrain, marked by algorithms and data, may seem daunting, but it is also ripe with opportunity. As we navigate this terrain, this book emphasizes the importance of intention and humanity. The goal is not to create classrooms that are mere extensions of ChatGPT but rather to foster environments where technology is harnessed to enrich human interaction, creativity, and empathy. When you are equipped with the right tools and knowledge, AI can become a powerful ally in the quest for a more enlightened and equitable education system.

We are at a pivotal moment in history—one that demands a reevaluation of the educator's role in an AI-infused future. The question now is how can we mold that relationship to reflect the values we hold dear in the teaching profession? *The AI Assist* seeks to answer this question, providing a scaffold upon which you can build a future that respects the delicate balance between technological advancement and the timeless value of human mentorship and guidance.

We'll embark on a mission to reconcile the technological surge of AI with the timeless craft of teaching. This is not a manifesto advocating for the replacement of educators with machines, nor is it a treatise pushing a technology-first doctrine. Instead, this book stands as an affirmation of AI's role as a powerful adjunct to the human efforts in education, capable of enriching student learning and broadening the horizons of what's possible in an inclusive, innovative, and impactful learning environment.

The HAIL model—Humanizing, Augmenting, Integrating, and Leveraging AI—is the bedrock upon which this book is built, championing the conviction that human connection, empathy, and creativity are the soul of education. These are the elements that no algorithm can replicate; they're the qualities that AI should aim to support and elevate. We will navigate these themes in an integrated manner, reflecting the fluidity with which AI should meld into the fabric of education. Each chapter highlights practical examples, reflective questions, and links to further resources, painting a comprehensive picture of AI's role in education.

This narrative is born from my experiences as a school and district administrator, where I piloted initiatives to weave technology into the fabric of our classrooms. It was a time of intense learning, and it was a challenge at times to fit the proverbial square peg of technology into the round hole of educational needs. Those experiences, coupled with the advent of AI, have reshaped the landscape of educational possibilities for me, bringing new opportunities and ethical considerations to the fore.

Parallels with the SAMR Model

To guide our thoughtful integration of AI in education, we can draw valuable insights from Ruben Puentedura's SAMR model (2013). This model provides a framework for educators to reflect on how they are incorporating technology into their teaching, with each level—Substitution, Augmentation, Modification, and Redefinition—offering a progressively more significant impact on teaching and learning outcomes.

I urge you, as an educator, to see AI as a multifaceted instrument—akin to how the SAMR model encourages educators to progress beyond merely substituting traditional methods with digital counterparts. AI, when aligned with this model, can augment your teaching by providing immediate feedback to students, thereby enhancing the learning process. Further, it can modify your approach to education by facilitating new ways of interacting and engaging with content that were previously inconceivable. Ultimately, AI has the potential to redefine education by creating entirely new methods of learning and collaboration, propelled by its data-driven insights and adaptive capabilities.

Before we delve into the intersection of AI and this model, let's take a moment to unpack each layer of SAMR in detail. The first level, Substitution, is where technology acts as a straightforward swap for traditional tools, without enhancing the learning experience. Think of it as reading an ebook instead of a paperback—the medium changes, but the act of reading remains the same. Augmentation, the second level, still replaces the old with the new but with added benefits; for example, a digital thesaurus can suggest synonyms quickly, enriching a student's vocabulary as they write.

The Modification level is where true transformation begins. Here, technology fundamentally changes the task. Imagine students using collaborative online documents to work together in real time, breaking the confines of the classroom walls and enabling a more dynamic learning process. Finally, Redefinition takes us to the peak, where technology allows for brand-new, previously impossible tasks to emerge. Consider students using simulation software to conduct virtual science experiments, allowing for infinite repetitions and manipulations without the constraints of physical lab time or resources.

Just as Puentedura's model advocates for transformative uses of technology in education, I invite you to harness AI in ways that not only change the shape of tasks but also transform pedagogical strategies and learner outcomes. This approach is not about allowing technology to overshadow the human elements of teaching but having technology support and elevate them, promoting a balance that fosters a rich learning community.

The ultimate aim is to integrate AI in a manner that respects and amplifies our shared humanity. This approach involves using AI to bring forth a deeper understanding of subject matter and to tailor educational experiences to each learner's unique needs and aspirations. The role of AI here is not to supplant the teacher but to serve as a dynamic and responsive tool, enhancing the teacher's ability to connect with and inspire students.

In your journey as an educator in this AI-infused landscape, remember that, like the SAMR model, the use of AI should be a deliberate choice aimed at improving instruction and outcomes. Consider AI's role at each level of the SAMR ladder and strive to push beyond substitution toward transformative teaching experiences. Embrace AI as a partner in the education process—one that brings new dimensions to teaching and learning and opens doors to experiences that prepare students for an increasingly complex and technology-integrated world.

In this light, your approach to AI integration becomes a dance between technology and pedagogy, choreographed with intention and guided by a model that values both innovation and the irreplaceable human touch.

Using the HAIL Model

As you progress through this book, you'll gain increasingly valuable insights into applying the HAIL model. The strategies provided are ready for implementation in your classroom and supported by practical examples and reflective prompts that challenge you to think deeper. This comprehensive approach is designed to equip you, the educator, with the tools needed to chart a course through the evolving landscape of AI in education—a landscape in which human touch remains paramount and AI serves as a tool to enhance the tapestry we continue to weave.

The HAIL model's beauty lies in its ability to be not merely a static framework but a living spectrum that evolves and adapts, reflecting the multifaceted and dynamic nature of today's classrooms. Recognizing that educators hail from diverse backgrounds, face unique challenges, and teach students with a wide array of needs and aspirations, the model offers fluidity. It acts as a guide, empowering you to fine-tune your strategies and ensure that AI integration is not just effective but also personal and tailored to your classroom's specific tapestry.

Embracing the HAIL model as a continuum acknowledges that planning with AI in education isn't a one-size-fits-all approach; it's about sliding along a scale that ranges from enriching human connection to leveraging sophisticated AI tools. This scale provides a flexible approach to planning, allowing you to adjust the mix of human and AI elements in response to the shifting landscape.

The HAIL continuum balances forward-thinking vision with practical realism. While exploring AI's potential to revolutionize education, I acknowledge the everyday challenges you face. This continuum serves as your guide, illuminating the path ahead while anchoring you to education's core mission: fostering human connections, nurturing understanding, and promoting student growth.

The HAIL continuum starts with Humanize, emphasizing the non-negotiable value of the human touch—empathy and understanding—within the learning process. This principle affirms teaching as an art that goes beyond curricula, embracing human emotions, connections, and experiences and valuing each student's individual path.

Moving to Augment, the continuum delves into enhancing our capabilities with AI's support, striking a delicate balance where technology amplifies the strengths of our educational methods without compromising the personal connection that is the hallmark of great teaching.

The Integrate phase smoothly blends AI tools with established teaching methods. Here, technology enhances our teaching practices, enriching learning while preserving the educator's unique influence.

Leverage represents the forefront of AI-driven education. This phase encourages you to fully utilize AI's capabilities to customize learning, predict needs, and transform students from passive learners into active participants in a dynamic education environment.

The HAIL model thus evolves from theory to practice. It guides you through education's changing landscape, providing the knowledge and tools to effectively combine AI innovations with traditional teaching methods.

How This Book Is Structured

This book's chapters form the core of our exploration—each one is a stepping stone on your journey to integrating AI into education with skill and insight:

Chapter 1: Understanding the Context: We begin by delving deep into the dynamics of your classroom. This chapter is about understanding the unique blend of personalities, learning styles, and existing tech landscape that make up your environment. It's about setting the stage for AI integration that's thoughtful and effective, taking into account your students' diverse needs and capabilities.

Chapter 2: Identifying Goals and Needs: Here, you'll be encouraged to clearly articulate what you aim to achieve with AI in your classroom. Is it enhancing student engagement, personalizing learning, or perhaps streamlining administrative tasks? This chapter helps you set meaningful, achievable objectives, ensuring that the technology you integrate serves a clear, beneficial purpose in your instruction.

Chapter 3: Selecting Appropriate AI Tools: With goals in hand, this chapter explores how to choose the right AI tools. It's not just about what's new or popular; it's about what aligns with your education objectives, your classroom's unique needs, and your personal teaching style. Learn to navigate the burgeoning market of educational technology with a discerning eye, selecting tools that will truly augment and amplify the learning experience.

Chapter 4: Planning and Designing Activities: Now it's time to roll up your sleeves and start designing AI-enhanced lesson plans. This chapter guides you through integrating AI into your curriculum in a way that's seamless and effective. You'll find strategies for marrying technological sophistication with depth, ensuring that every activity is enriching, engaging, and pedagogically sound.

Chapter 5: Implementing AI-Enhanced Activities in the Classroom: Once the planning is done, the real action begins. This chapter offers practical advice for bringing your AI-enhanced activities to life in the classroom. From the logistics of setup and introduction to strategies for keeping students engaged and on track, you'll find a treasure trove of tips for making your AI activities a success. This is also where you'll learn to be agile, monitoring student responses and being ready to adapt as needed.

Chapter 6: Assessment and Reflection on AI-Enhanced Learning: After implementation comes reflection. This critical chapter focuses on your AI integration's effectiveness and the impact it has on student learning. It's about developing a cycle of continuous improvement, where each iteration of AI use in your classroom is informed by the last. You'll learn methods for assessing both student progress and your own teaching, using these insights to refine and enhance your approach.

Chapter 7: Fostering a Culture of Continuous Improvement in AI Integration: Commit to ongoing enhancement of your AI-integrated teaching practice. This chapter is about cultivating a mindset of perpetual growth and adaptability. You're encouraged to view each lesson—each interaction with technology—as an opportunity to learn and evolve. Dive into the iterative process of refining your AI integration, drawing from student feedback, emerging AI tools, and the latest in professional development. Learn to embrace change as the only constant, using it to fuel your pursuit of education excellence. This chapter guides you in maintaining innovative teaching practices, ensuring that AI thoughtfully enhances both your instruction and your students' learning experiences.

Each chapter aims to inform, inspire, and empower you. As you begin integrating AI into your teaching, remember: This isn't just about adopting new technology. It's about advancing the fundamental education goal of fostering knowledge and understanding.

The HAIL model guides you throughout this book, offering direction whether you're new to AI or experienced in education technology. It reflects my conviction that AI can improve education while addressing real classroom challenges. The model helps you navigate the many possibilities AI offers in education.

Connections to the ISTE Standards

In each chapter, you'll find connections to the ISTE Educator Standards. Just as the chapters identify stepping stones on your journey to integrating AI tools into your human-centered instruction, the ISTE Educator Standards provide a road map to help students become empowered learners. These standards will deepen your practice, promote collaboration with peers, challenge you to rethink traditional approaches, and help you prepare students to drive their own learning. Explore the ISTE Educator Standards in full here: https://iste.org/standards/educators.

A Practical Guide for the Educator

In the upcoming chapters, you'll find lesson plans that apply the HAIL model, demonstrating how human interaction and AI can seamlessly work together in the classroom. The principles of this model emphasize the crucial role of human connection alongside AI's powerful capabilities, setting the stage for their integrated use in education.

At the core of this practical approach is the sliding-scale concept, an adaptable framework that goes beyond theory. This model empowers you to balance your essential human insights with the data-driven perspectives that AI technologies provide, ensuring your teaching methods meet the evolving needs of today's classrooms.

Imagine the HAIL model as a spectrum, with Humanize and Leverage at opposite ends and Augment and Integrate in between. Like a pianist selecting the right keys to create a fitting melody, educators can choose the appropriate approach for each learning situation. This flexible model allows teachers to tailor their methods—whether that means emphasizing human connection, personal narratives, or leveraging AI's customized feedback—to best suit the needs of their students and the subject matter.

The continuum's vitality lies in its versatility. It is not about adhering to rigid benchmarks or ticking off criteria. Rather, it serves as an advisory, shedding light on the wide array of options educators have at their disposal. Whether it's deploying a novel AI application or deepening human relationships within a technologically advanced lesson, the sliding scale provides guidance and support, aligning with each lesson's unique needs and the learners' varied necessities.

The sliding scale advocates a balanced stance, avoiding any overreliance on either extremity. By recognizing the placement of a particular teaching session or activity along this continuum, educators are equipped to make judicious decisions, ensuring that neither the human factor is eclipsed nor the potential of AI is underleveraged.

Why is such dynamism crucial? Classrooms are far from being monolithic; they're dynamic ecosystems brimming with students who bring a plethora of experiences, learning speeds, and levels of understanding. The sliding-scale concept acknowledges and embraces this heterogeneity, enabling educators to adjust and refine their instructional methods dynamically. This ensures that each student connects with the lessons, feels acknowledged, and stays actively involved, regardless of their starting point.

Delving deeper into the HAIL model's pragmatic use reveals that the synergy of human insight and AI is not solely about the incorporation of technology. It's a conscious, nuanced blend, guaranteeing that every teaching moment, activity, or project is imbued with the sincerity of human interaction, amplified by the precision and flexibility of AI. The sliding scale acts as a navigational tool on this voyage, steering educators toward developing comprehensive, equitable, and forward-thinking learning experiences for every student.

1

Understanding the Context

ISTE EDUCATOR STANDARDS

2.1.a: Educators set professional learning goals to apply teaching practices made possible by technology, explore promising innovations, and reflect on their effectiveness.

2.2.b: Educators advocate for equitable access to technology, high-quality digital content, and learning opportunities to meet the diverse needs of all students.

2.3.b: Educators foster digital literacy by encouraging curiosity, reflection, and the critical evaluation of digital resources.

You're at the intersection of established teaching methods and innovative technology. Your task is to comprehensively assess your classroom's unique environment—including each student, the available technology, and your current teaching strategies: all of which can be enhanced by AI. Reflect on the effectiveness of technology-integrated pedagogy (Standard 2.1.a) as you consider how AI can augment and transform learning experiences, ensuring that the technology serves pedagogical goals, not just technical possibilities.

I challenge you to map the terrain of your classroom meticulously. This includes recognizing your students' individuality, acknowledging the variety of ways they learn, and understanding the technological framework that supports your efforts. Advocate for equitable access to educational technology (Standard 2.3.b) to ensure that each student has the opportunity to benefit from AI-enhanced learning, addressing the digital divide that might limit some students' educational experiences.

This pursuit of understanding transcends mere academic knowledge; it calls for empathy, inviting you as an educator to inhabit your learners' perspectives and grasp the multitude of ways they engage with knowledge and technology. To achieve this deep understanding, utilize a blend of surveys to capture student voices, direct observation to see the interplay in action, and conduct thorough reviews of the technological tools at your disposal. These are not just procedural checks; they are the means to an essential end: a detailed and empathetic understanding of your classroom, crucial for a seamless and effective integration of AI.

Studies have shown that students' prior experiences with adaptive learning tools positively correlates with their acceptance of AI integration in the classroom (Schroeder et al., 2022). When AI enters this space, it should not diminish the human aspect but enrich it, making the educational experience more efficient, resonant, and meaningful.

In this exploration, you will engage with the HAIL model, which is not merely a static set of principles but a dynamic guide that adapts to the evolving needs of your classroom. Establish a culture for critical examination of online resources, promoting digital literacy (Standard 2.2.b) as you and your students navigate the wealth of information available online. Throughout this chapter, you will delve into practical applications and real-life scenarios that illustrate the nuanced integration of AI in education. You will consider the ethical dimensions, the pedagogical consequences, and the practical challenges of bringing AI into your teaching practice. In addition, you will approach these considerations with precision and clarity, ensuring that the insights you gather are deeply rooted in the tangible experience of day-to-day teaching.

Integrating AI into education requires looking past data to recognize each student's unique qualities and needs. This process involves exploration and empathy, aiming to create a learning experience that balances technological advancement with human connection.

Surveys and Data Collection

The craft of effective surveying lies in carefully constructing questions that elicit not only the preferences and experiences of the respondents but also their concerns and aspirations regarding technology in education. Figures 1.1 and 1.2 show how you might approach these surveys.

FIGURE 1.1

Student Technology Survey Template

1. **Demographics**
   - Grade level:
   - Age range:
   - Access to internet at home (Y/N):
2. **Technology Usage**
   - Which devices do you regularly use? (e.g., smartphone, tablet, laptop, desktop)
   - How comfortable do you feel using technology in your learning? (scale of 1–5)
   - What types of technology do you use for schoolwork? (e.g., educational apps, search engines, ebooks)
3. **Experience with AI**
   - Have you used tools that change or adapt based on your input? (e.g., learning apps that get harder as you get answers right)
   - How do you feel about using technology that can learn and adapt to help you study?
4. **Learning Preferences**
   - Do you prefer learning with technology, with a teacher, or a mix of both? Why?
   - What subjects do you think might benefit from the use of AI or technology?
5. **Concerns and Expectations**
   - What concerns do you have about using AI in the classroom?
   - What do you hope AI technology will help you with in your learning?

FIGURE 1.2

Parent Technology Survey Template

1. **Demographics**
    - Number of school-age children:
    - Do you have a reliable internet connection at home? (Y/N)
2. **Observations of Your Child's Learning**
    - Have you noticed your child using technology for learning at home? Can you provide examples?
    - How does your child respond to using technology for their homework or projects?
3. **Attitudes Toward AI and Technology in Education**
    - How do you feel about the use of AI and technology in your child's education?
    - Do you have any particular concerns about your child's use of technology or AI for learning?
4. **Support and Engagement**
    - Would you be interested in learning more about how AI can support your child's education? (Y/N)
    - What types of support would you find helpful for integrating technology into your child's learning at home?
5. **Expectations from the School**
    - What are your expectations from the school when it comes to using AI and technology in your child's education?
    - How would you like to be informed or involved in decisions related to technology use in the classroom?

Data Analysis Approach for Educators

The following steps outline a structured approach for you, the educator, to sift through the collected data, discern patterns, and understand the deeper stories these patterns reveal. With this comprehensive analysis, you are equipped to make informed decisions that resonate with both the art and science of teaching in an AI-enhanced classroom.

Step 1: Organize Your Data

Collect and sort responses. To gather and organize survey responses, follow these steps:

1. Choose a data entry tool. Depending on the complexity of your survey and the volume of responses, you can use various tools. Here are a few options:
   a. Use spreadsheet software: Use programs like Microsoft Excel or Google Sheets. These are excellent for entering, organizing, and analyzing survey data.
   b. Use survey software: Online survey tools such as SurveyMonkey, Google Forms, or Typeform usually offer built-in data export options.
2. Set up your spreadsheet.
   a. Create columns for each question: In your spreadsheet, set up columns where each column represents a different survey question.
   b. Input responses: Manually input each respondent's answers into the corresponding columns. If you have many responses, consider using a form linked to the spreadsheet for easier data entry.
3. Use survey software.
   a. Export data: Most survey tools allow you to export collected responses directly into a spreadsheet format like Excel or CSV.
   b. Download and open: Download the exported file and open it in your spreadsheet software for further analysis.
4. Organize your data.
   a. Label columns clearly: Ensure that each column is labeled with the corresponding question for easy reference.
   b. Ensure consistent formatting: Use consistent data formats (e.g., text, numbers, dates) to facilitate easier analysis.
5. Create in Excel or Google Sheets.
   a. Create a header row: Label columns A1, B1, C1, and so on with the questions from your survey.
   b. Input data: Start from row 2 and enter each respondent's answers in the corresponding cells.

By organizing your data in a structured format, you can easily analyze the responses and generate insights from your survey.

Step 2: Look for Basic Patterns

Count responses. For multiple-choice and scale questions, count how many times each response was chosen. This can often be done using the sort and count functions in spreadsheet software.

Notice extremes. Spot any answers that stand out, such as if almost everyone or almost no one is comfortable with a certain type of technology.

Step 3: Understand the Stories Behind the Numbers

Read open-ended responses. Take time to read through the answers to open-ended questions. Highlight any comments that come up often or that are particularly powerful or surprising.

Group similar comments. Put similar comments together to see what themes emerge. For example, group all the concerns about AI together to see what worries people most.

Step 4: Combine Numbers and Stories

Connect the dots. Look for ways the numbers from your multiple-choice questions might explain the stories from your open-ended answers. For example, if many students don't have internet at home, does this relate to concerns about being able to complete homework?

Make notes. Write down any connections you find. These notes will be helpful when you make decisions about using AI in your classroom.

Step 5: Share What You've Found

Create a simple report. Summarize what you've learned. Include how many people gave each kind of answer for your scale or multiple-choice questions, and then list the main themes you found in the open-ended responses.

Discuss with colleagues. Share your findings with other teachers, administrators, or even students and parents to get their perspectives.

Step 6: Plan Your Next Steps with the HAIL Model in Mind

Identify needs according to the HAIL model. Reflect on your findings in light of the Humanize, Augment, Integrate, and Leverage aspects of the HAIL model. For instance, if students need more basic tech skills (Humanize), plan for introductory sessions that build digital literacy. If they're showing readiness for more advanced AI tools (Leverage), consider exploring AI applications that offer deeper analytics or personalized learning experiences.

Align AI integration with classroom dynamics. Use the survey data to understand where your class currently fits within the HAIL continuum. If there's a high comfort level with tech, you might be more toward the Integrate and Leverage end. If comfort is lower, focus on Humanize and Augment strategies to build confidence and skills gradually.

Consider resources and constraints. Take stock of the technological resources available to you and the constraints you face. This will influence how you move along the HAIL continuum. For example, limited access to devices might mean focusing on Humanize strategies, such as using AI for group discussions, whereas abundant resources might allow for a full Leverage approach with individualized AI learning plans.

Customize the approach. Tailor the use of AI tools to fit the unique blend of your classroom's needs. If your data show that students are diverse in their tech comfort, create a plan that allows for different entry points into AI use, ensuring that no student is left behind.

Prepare for professional development. Based on the survey, identify areas where you or your colleagues might need professional development to better integrate AI into the classroom. This is an essential step to ensure that AI tools are used effectively and to their full potential.

Step 7: Reflect and Adjust

Engage in trial and error. Make a plan based on what you've learned and try it out. See how it goes and be ready to make changes.

Ask for feedback. After trying out AI in your classroom, ask your students what they think. Did it help? What could make it better?

By following these steps, you can analyze survey data in a practical and nontechnical way. This approach will help you make informed decisions about integrating AI into your classroom in a way that's responsive to your students' needs and capabilities. Remember, the survey's purpose is not to validate a predetermined decision to use AI but to genuinely understand your classroom community's readiness for and attitudes toward such integration. The insights gathered here will directly inform the choice of tools, the pace of integration, and the necessary support structures that need to be put in place.

Observational Studies

Observational studies are a cornerstone of understanding how AI technology integrates into the classroom environment. These studies provide educators with invaluable, real-time insights into the nuanced interactions between students and technology. Unlike surveys or controlled experiments, observational studies capture the authentic, unscripted moments that occur when students engage with AI tools in their natural learning environment. This method allows educators to witness firsthand how students navigate, struggle with, and benefit from AI-enhanced learning experiences. By carefully observing these interactions, teachers can identify patterns, challenges, and opportunities that might not be apparent through other forms of assessment. These studies are particularly crucial in the early stages of AI integration, as they can reveal unexpected uses of the technology, highlight areas where students need additional support, and showcase the most effective applications of AI in enhancing the learning process. When conducting these studies, educators should approach the task with a structured yet open-minded perspective, ready to document both the anticipated and unforeseen aspects of AI's impact on student learning and engagement. The following guidelines will help ensure that your observational studies yield rich, actionable insights:

- **Plan the observation.** Decide what you're looking for. Is it how students work together using technology? How they solve problems with AI assistance? How they manage distractions?
- **Use a checklist.** Create a checklist to record specific behaviors, such as time on task, expressions of frustration, instances of collaboration, or "aha!" moments.

- **Look for nonverbal cues.** Pay attention to body language. Are students leaning in, indicating engagement, or are they slouching and looking away from the screen?
- **Take notes on context.** Record the context in which behaviors occur. Is a student's disengagement due to the technology itself or an unrelated classroom disruption?
- **Reflect on equity.** Observe whether all students have equal access to and participation with the technology. Note any disparities that could inform future AI integration efforts.

After observations, educators should analyze their notes, looking for patterns and considering the implications for future technology use. If certain technologies, such as AI-driven interactive learning platforms (e.g., DreamBox) or adaptive learning systems (e.g., Smart Sparrow), consistently elicit positive engagement, then they might be ripe for AI augmentation. For instance, DreamBox provides personalized math lessons that adapt in real time based on student input, offering a dynamic and responsive learning experience. Similarly, Smart Sparrow allows for the creation of adaptive learning pathways in various subjects, providing immediate feedback and content tailored to each learner's needs.

Conversely, if technology is causing anxiety or distraction, a different approach may be necessary. For example, if students find AI chatbots like Replika or conversational agents like Mitsuku overwhelming, it might be beneficial to start with more foundational digital skills development. Begin with simpler, more intuitive tools such as Khan Academy, which offers structured lessons and straightforward practice exercises without the complexity of adaptive AI. Once students are comfortable with these foundational tools, gradually introduce more advanced AI applications.

Case Studies and Anecdotal Evidence

Incorporating case studies into the decision-making process can provide a road map for AI integration and preemptively address potential challenges. Here are steps for finding and using case studies effectively.

Example Case Study: Knewton and AI

Knewton, an adaptive learning technology platform, uses AI to personalize educational content. By analyzing students' interactions and performance data, Knewton tailors lessons to each learner's needs, optimizing their experience. For instance, if a student struggles with a specific math concept, Knewton provides additional resources and practice problems targeting that area, whereas students who demonstrate proficiency can advance to more challenging material. This adaptive approach helps ensure that all students receive the appropriate level of support and challenge, enhancing engagement and learning outcomes.

Success and Impact: Knewton demonstrated its effectiveness in a study with more than 10,000 students, showing that mastery of subjects through its program correlated with improved overall course performance. This impact was especially pronounced for students who were struggling with foundational concepts in subjects like mathematics and science. For instance, in mathematics, Knewton provided customized practice problems and instructional content to address specific gaps in understanding. In science, the platform offered tailored lessons and quizzes to reinforce key concepts. By targeting these areas of difficulty, Knewton helped students build a stronger foundation, ultimately assisting in closing education gaps and enhancing overall academic performance.

Technology and Approach: At the heart of Knewton's system is an AI algorithm trained with extensive data to identify knowledge gaps and optimize content delivery. The platform acquires most of its content from open resources, reducing costs for students while allowing for significant scalability and customization.

Challenges and Evolution: Despite its initial success, Knewton faced challenges, including skepticism over its "black box" approach and competition from integrated players in the education market. Its acquisition by Wiley marked a new chapter, strengthening its position with access to additional resources and credibility in the education sector.

Research and collect. Look for case studies on educational technology websites, in academic journals, or through professional networks. Many organizations publish their findings on AI projects in schools.

Analyze the case studies. Identify the objectives, implementation strategies, results, and reflections provided in the case studies. Pay close attention to the context to see how closely it mirrors your own.

Compare and contrast. Consider how the outcomes of these studies align with the data and observations from your classroom. Are there similarities in student engagement or teacher feedback?

Extract lessons. Draw out key lessons from these cases. For example, a case study might reveal the importance of teacher training in successful AI integration or highlight strategies that foster student agency.

Adapt and apply. Use the insights gained to inform your approach. Perhaps a study shows that gradual implementation of AI tools led to better outcomes, suggesting the need to pace their integration in your classroom.

Application to the HAIL Model

- **Humanize:** Knewton's approach aligns with the Humanize aspect by addressing individual student needs and preferences, allowing learners to progress at their own pace and style. It acknowledges the human aspect of learning by adapting to each student's unique learning journey.
- **Augment:** By providing personalized recommendations and adapting content based on student performance, Knewton augments the process, enhancing the capabilities of both students and educators.
- **Integrate:** The platform exemplifies the Integrate aspect by seamlessly incorporating AI into the learning experience without replacing the educator. Instead, it serves as a tool that educators can use to understand students' needs better and tailor their teaching strategies.
- **Leverage:** Finally, Knewton demonstrates the Leverage aspect by making use of AI's full potential to transform the learning experience. It leverages data-driven insights to create a more effective and personalized learning environment.

By understanding and applying the lessons we can learn from Knewton, educators and institutions can better navigate the complexities of AI integration in general, aligning with the principles of the HAIL model to create a balanced, student-centered approach to learning. In addition, by engaging with both observational studies and case studies, educators can develop a nuanced understanding of how AI might fit into their classrooms. This understanding can guide a responsive and informed approach to technology integration, ensuring that it enhances the experience for all students.

Educational Technology Resources Review

A thorough review starts with a comprehensive inventory of all hardware and software currently used in instruction. This includes listing devices like computers, tablets, and interactive whiteboards and noting their specifications, age, and condition. Similarly, documenting all software and online platforms, especially those that are AI driven, is crucial. This inventory should also assess the quality of internet access available because AI applications often require strong and stable connections. Understanding the current technological infrastructure's capabilities and limitations is key to determining the school's readiness for further AI integration.

The effectiveness of AI tools is significantly influenced by the user's ability to operate them. Therefore, assessing the training that staff have received on existing technology and AI tools is essential. Identifying gaps in knowledge or skills will highlight areas where additional professional development is needed. Alongside training, the availability and quality of technical support for both hardware and software issues are vital components of successful AI integration, ensuring that any technical issues can be addressed promptly and effectively.

Ensuring equitable access to technology is fundamental to preparing for AI integration. This means ensuring that all students have the necessary devices and that the software is accessible to students with different needs. An assessment of students' digital literacy levels is also crucial because this will determine the kind of instruction or support needed for students to effectively engage with AI tools. This aspect of the review will help you understand how ready your students are for AI-enhanced learning and what measures need to be taken to support them.

To assess students' digital skills, teachers can use various resources and tools, such as the following examples. These resources provide a variety of ways to assess and support students' digital literacy, ensuring that they are prepared to effectively engage with AI-enhanced learning tools.

1. **Common Sense Education's Digital Citizenship Curriculum:** This offers a comprehensive set of lessons and assessments to help evaluate students' digital literacy and citizenship skills.
2. **Northstar Digital Literacy Assessment:** This is an online tool that provides assessments for basic computer skills, internet use, email, and more. Teachers can use this resource to gauge students' digital competencies.
3. **ISTE Student Standards:** The International Society for Technology in Education (ISTE) provides guidelines and assessment tools to help educators evaluate students' proficiency with technology.
4. **Google's Applied Digital Skills:** This is a free online curriculum that includes video-based lessons on a variety of digital skills, with integrated assessments to help teachers track student progress.
5. **Microsoft Digital Literacy Curriculum:** This offers a range of modules and assessments to help students build and demonstrate their digital literacy skills.

It should be noted that integrating AI into education comes with a host of legal and ethical considerations, primarily regarding data privacy and security. A review must include a thorough understanding of the data privacy policies of all AI tools and software in use, ensuring compliance with laws and regulations such as the General Data Protection Regulation (GDPR) and the Children's Online Privacy Protection Act (COPPA). Security measures for physical devices and cybersecurity must be evaluated to protect sensitive information.

Additionally, the ethical implications of AI use, including issues of bias, transparency, and the overall impact on student learning and autonomy, should be considered and addressed.

Educators need to think and talk about the following key questions and issues:

1. Data Privacy and Security
    a. What specific data are the AI tools collecting?
    b. How are these data stored and who has access to it?
    c. Are there clear policies in place to protect student data and ensure compliance with GDPR, COPPA, and other relevant regulations?
    d. What cybersecurity measures are in place to prevent data breaches and protect sensitive information?
2. Bias in AI
    a. How are the AI algorithms trained, and is there a risk of bias in the data sets used?
    b. What measures are in place to identify and mitigate bias in AI tools?
    c. How can educators ensure that AI does not reinforce existing inequalities or stereotypes?
3. Transparency and Accountability
    a. Are the AI tools' decision-making processes transparent to educators, students, and parents?
    b. How can educators explain AI decisions and recommendations to students and parents in an understandable way?
    c. Who is accountable if an AI tool makes a mistake or negatively affects student learning?
4. Impact on Student Learning and Autonomy
    a. How does the use of AI tools affect students' learning experiences and outcomes?
    b. Are AI tools enhancing or hindering students' critical thinking and problem-solving skills?
    c. What steps can be taken to ensure that AI tools support student autonomy rather than create dependency?

By addressing these questions and issues, educators can ensure that the integration of AI into education is not only effective but also ethical and equitable, fostering a learning environment that respects and promotes all students' well-being and development.

As technology rapidly evolves, it's important to consider the longevity and adaptability of the current technological infrastructure. Assessing the upgradability and scalability of current technology is essential in planning for the future. This includes considering how easily current technology can be upgraded or replaced and whether the infrastructure can accommodate the increasing demands of more advanced AI applications. Planning for future needs ensures that the school remains equipped and ready for ongoing technological advancements.

By undertaking this comprehensive review with a collaborative and continuous improvement approach, schools can ensure that they are not only ready for current AI integration but also well prepared for future advancements. This review should become a regular part of the institution's technology planning, involving a team of stakeholders and leading to a clear action plan based on the findings. With a thorough understanding of their technological landscape, education institutions can create effective, safe, and equitable AI-enhanced learning environments.

Bridging a systematic review and practical applications requires seeing AI integration as an ongoing process of innovation in education. This view allows you to anticipate trends while addressing current needs. Moving from assessing AI readiness to implementing the tools demands continuous learning and flexibility.

The period between review and application is crucial for developing ideas. Use this time to reflect on findings, consider potential uses, and align AI tools with the HAIL model. Here, theory transforms into actionable plans.

Our real-world examples show AI's potential to transform education when used thoughtfully. These cases represent a broader shift in education—one that is informed by data and the actual experiences of teachers and students. They also demonstrate how AI can expand learning opportunities in novel ways when grounded in an education context.

Real-World Examples

Let's examine some practical applications of the HAIL model in different classroom settings. These examples show how to integrate AI effectively across various subjects and learning environments. We'll explore specific scenarios in STEM, language arts, and diverse classrooms, demonstrating how to apply each component of the HAIL model: Humanize, Augment, Integrate, and Leverage. These real-world cases provide concrete strategies you can adapt for your own classroom, illustrating how AI can enhance traditional teaching methods, personalize learning, and address diverse student needs. Use these examples as a starting point to reimagine your own teaching practices with AI.

1. STEM Classroom: Virtual Lab Simulations
   - **Humanize:** Initiate the lab with a discussion on how technology can enhance understanding and simulate real-world scenarios, emphasizing the value of personal exploration in science.
   - **Augment:** The virtual lab, such as those provided by platforms like Labster or PhET Interactive Simulations, augments traditional lab equipment by providing simulations of experiments that are otherwise too dangerous, expensive, or impossible in a school setting.
   - **Integrate:** Seamlessly blend the virtual lab into your existing curriculum, using it not as a standalone tool but as a complement to traditional methods. For example, use virtual simulations to prepare students for hands-on lab work or to explore scenarios impossible in a physical lab. This integration creates a more comprehensive learning experience, where digital and traditional approaches reinforce each other.
   - **Leverage:** Utilize the AI's ability to analyze student performance, adapt challenges accordingly, and provide personalized learning paths. For example, if a student demonstrates proficiency in a specific concept, the AI can introduce more advanced topics, or it can offer additional support and practice to those who struggle, thereby ensuring individualized education tailored to each student's ability and goals.

2. Language Arts Classroom: AI-Assisted Writing Workshops
   - **Humanize:** Begin with a face-to-face workshop where students share their writing goals and challenges. Discuss how AI tools can support their individual growth as writers, emphasizing that the technology is there to enhance, not replace, their unique voice and creativity.
   - **Augment:** The AI tool, such as Grammarly or ProWritingAid, augments the writing process by offering real-time, actionable feedback, allowing students to improve their skills incrementally.
   - **Integrate:** Make the AI writing assistant a standard part of the writing process. For example, have students use the AI tool to review their first draft, then bring the AI-suggested edits to peer review sessions for discussion. This blends AI feedback with human critique and reflection.
   - **Leverage:** Leverage AI to provide a level of individualized attention and feedback that would be impossible for a teacher to provide alone, especially in larger classes. This means that each student receives personalized feedback tailored to their specific writing challenges, helping them improve more effectively.
3. Diverse Classroom: Adaptive Reading Circles
   - **Humanize:** Begin with in-person book discussions where students share their interpretations and personal connections to the text. Emphasize the value of diverse perspectives and encourage empathy through storytelling, setting a foundation of human connection before introducing technology.
   - **Augment:** Introduce an adaptive reading platform that suggests texts matching each student's reading level. Use this to support diverse learning needs, allowing students to access content that challenges them appropriately while still participating in group discussions about common themes.
   - **Integrate:** Incorporate the adaptive reading tools into daily classroom routines. For instance, use AI-generated reading comprehension questions for warm-up activities or have students use the platform

to find supporting evidence for their arguments during discussions. This makes the AI tool a seamless part of the learning process.

- **Leverage:** Utilize the AI's data analysis capabilities to create personalized learning pathways for each student. For example, use AI to identify specific reading skills each student needs to improve (such as inferencing or vocabulary acquisition), automatically generate targeted exercises, and adjust the difficulty of texts in real time based on student performance. Use these data to inform your teaching strategies and provide individualized support.

These examples from various contexts demonstrate how AI can be progressively integrated into education, from humanizing the learning experience to leveraging AI's full capabilities. Each stage of the HAIL model offers unique benefits; when combined, they provide a comprehensive approach to incorporating AI in education that is sensitive to human needs and maximizes the potential of technology.

Empowering Your Path to AI Integration

I hope you feel equipped with a robust methodology to understand and navigate your classroom's unique dynamics. My aim in this chapter has been to provide you with the insight necessary to integrate AI in a way that honors the individuality of each student and the collective spirit of your classroom community. Here's how this journey empowers you to move forward.

You've seen how surveys can serve as a mirror, reflecting the varied perspectives and readiness of your students and their families toward technology. These data aren't just numbers; they form the voice of your classroom community, guiding you to make informed and empathetic decisions. Your observational studies are more than a glance into classroom interactions; they are an opportunity to understand the subtle nuances of how students engage with technology. As you watch and note, you're gathering the threads of insight that will help you weave a more responsive and engaging learning environment.

2

Identifying Goals and Needs

ISTE EDUCATOR STANDARDS

2.1.c: Stay current with research that supports improved student learning outcomes, including findings from the learning sciences.
2.6.a: Foster a culture where students take ownership of their learning goals and outcomes in both independent and group settings.
2.7.a: Provide alternative ways for students to demonstrate competency and reflect on their learning using technology.

As you move from understanding your classroom's diverse makeup to visualizing its transformation through artificial intelligence, this chapter challenges you to define precise objectives for integrating AI into your instruction. You should also encourage students to take ownership of their learning goals in digital environments (Standard 2.6.a), emphasizing the self-directed exploration and the customization that AI can offer to suit their individual learning paths.

This goes beyond a simple fascination with new technology; it represents a strategic effort to utilize AI's capabilities to meet distinct, meaningful goals that substantially improve the quality and impact of learning experiences. It's key to provide alternative ways for students to demonstrate competency with technology (Standard 2.7.a), such as through interactive simulations or digital portfolios, ensuring that assessments capture a full range of student abilities and learning styles.

Consider this an invitation to shift your perspective—to see AI not as an end but as a means to enrich, diversify, and deepen education. Reflect on your classroom's multifaceted nature—its unique mix of challenges and strengths, aspirations and needs. Ask yourself how AI can address these various elements, and stay current with research supporting improved learning outcomes (Standard 2.1.c) to inform your strategies and ensure that the integration of AI into your classroom is informed by the latest findings and best practices in educational technology.

When articulating your aims, use the HAIL model as a framework to thoughtfully integrate AI into your instructional strategy:

Humanize: Begin with goals that center on human interaction and emotional intelligence. For example, aim to use AI to free up time for more one-on-one student mentoring or to facilitate deeper class discussions.

Augment: Set objectives for enhancing your existing teaching methods with AI. This could include using AI-powered tools to provide instant feedback on assignments or generate personalized practice exercises.

Integrate: Develop goals for seamlessly blending AI into your daily teaching practices. For instance, aim to incorporate AI-driven analytics into your lesson planning process or use AI-generated content alongside traditional materials.

Leverage: Establish ambitious goals that fully utilize AI's capabilities to transform your instructional approach. This might involve creating entirely personalized learning pathways for each student or using predictive analytics to proactively address learning gaps.

Articulating your AI objectives requires both a reflective and proactive stance. It demands a deep understanding of the current environment and a visionary grasp of AI's potential. By establishing clear, meaningful objectives aligned with the HAIL model, you make sure that AI becomes a transformative element that aligns with your environment's core values and needs. This careful approach ensures that as you navigate toward the future, your steps are continuously guided by a commitment to profoundly and sustainably enhance learning experiences.

Begin by delving into the broader vision for your classroom, considering the aspirations you hold for your students and the learning environment you aim to cultivate. How can AI not only align with this vision but also act as a catalyst to propel it forward? Reflect on the enduring challenges you encounter daily, whether they pertain to student engagement, differentiated instruction, or the efficiency of your administrative tasks. These challenges, when addressed thoughtfully with AI, can transform the learning landscape into a more dynamic, responsive, and inclusive space.

Take, for instance, the issue of student engagement. Consider how AI might contribute to crafting more compelling, interactive educational experiences. This could involve using advanced tools like ChatGPT to generate personalized writing prompts, DALL-E to create unique visual aids, or Copilot to offer real-time coding assistance to students. Such tools provide immediate, tailored feedback, enhancing the learning process and making lessons more engaging and relevant. This could involve adaptive learning systems that customize content to each learner's skill level and interests, or it could include gamification approaches that render learning more immersive and gratifying. Imagine AI as a tool that introduces a novel layer of interaction and personalization to your teaching, making each lesson resonate more profoundly and captivatingly with every student.

Within this context, the work of Holmes and Tuomi (2022) provides a pertinent foundation for understanding the potential and limitations of AI in education. Their comprehensive review of AI applications in diverse learning environments underscores the significance of aligning technology with pedagogical goals and students' individual needs. By incorporating findings from such research, you can further refine your AI integration strategy to ensure that it is grounded in evidence-based practices that support effective and engaging learning experiences.

In terms of personalized learning paths, AI can be a game changer. It offers the ability to analyze vast amounts of data on students' learning styles, preferences, and performance, enabling you to craft individualized learning experiences that cater to each student's unique needs and pace. Imagine a classroom where every student's educational journey is finely tuned to their capabilities and goals—where no one is left behind and everyone is challenged just right.

Streamlining administrative tasks is another area where AI can have a significant impact. Educators often find themselves mired in paperwork, grading, and other repetitive tasks that consume precious time that could be better spent interacting with students. AI-powered tools can automate many of these tasks, from grading quizzes to organizing schedules, freeing you to focus more on teaching and less on bureaucracy. This shift can lead to more time for direct student interaction, collaborative projects, and personalized feedback, ultimately enhancing the quality of education provided.

As you consider integrating AI into your classroom, ensure your goals are as varied as the students you teach. Start by identifying specific needs in your classroom and set clear, measurable objectives to address them. Whether you're looking to boost student engagement, personalize learning, or streamline administrative tasks, each goal should make a meaningful impact on your education environment, making it more effective and engaging for everyone.

Create SMART Goals

To structure your goal-setting process with AI integration effectively, it's essential to use the SMART criteria: specific, measurable, achievable, relevant, and time-bound. This method ensures that each of your objectives is well-defined and actionable. What follows is a practical guide to apply each aspect of the SMART criteria to your AI goals, including suggested forms or templates that can help document and track these objectives.

Specific

Your goals should be clear and specific, outlining exactly what you expect to achieve. Instead of a vague objective like "improve student engagement," specify what aspect of engagement you want to improve, how AI will be used, and which students or classes it will affect. For example, "Integrate an AI-driven interactive storytelling tool to increase participation rates in 9th grade literature classes." Create a goal specification sheet for each objective, detailing the what, who, where, and why (see Figure 2.1).

This sheet is intended to be a dynamic document, updated and referred to throughout the planning and implementation process. It's a practical tool to ensure that each AI integration goal is well-defined, clearly communicated, and aligned with broader objectives. Make sure to keep it accessible and review it regularly with your team or stakeholders involved in the AI integration process.

FIGURE 2.1

Goal Specification Sheet

Objective Title:

Date:

Prepared by:

What (Specific Goal):

Description of the AI Integration Goal:

Provide a specific and clear description of the goal. For example, "Implement an AI-driven personalized learning platform to support individualized math instruction for 6th grade students."

Who (Target Group/Individuals):

Primary Beneficiaries:

Identify the primary group or individuals who will benefit from the AI integration. For example, "6th grade students," "English language learners," or "Science department faculty."

Responsible Parties:

List the individuals or teams responsible for implementing and overseeing the goal. Include roles and names if applicable.

Where (Context/Location):

(continued)

FIGURE 2.1 (*continued*)

Goal Specification Sheet

Implementation Setting:

Describe where the AI tool will be implemented. For example, "in all 6th grade math classrooms," "school library during study hours," or "through the school's online learning platform."

Resource Location:

Note where necessary resources, support, or information can be found or is needed.

Why (Relevance/Justification):

Alignment with Broader Objectives:

Explain how the goal aligns with broader objectives or specific needs in the classroom or school.

Expected Benefits:

Detail the expected outcomes and benefits of achieving this goal, such as improved engagement, higher test scores, or more efficient use of teacher time.

Additional Notes:

Any other relevant information, potential challenges, or considerations.

Measurable

Attach measurable indicators to your goals to track progress and success. Determine what data will evidence the achievement of the goal. For the above example, a measurable outcome could be "Achieve a 20 percent increase in class participation as reflected in student surveys and classroom observations."

The goal measurement tracker shown in Figure 2.2 is a living document, intended to be regularly updated and referred to as you implement your AI integration goal. It serves as a practical tool to ensure continuous

FIGURE 2.2

Goal Measurement Tracker

Objective Title:

Goal Overview:

Brief Description:

Measurement Indicators:

List of Indicators:

Specify the key performance indicators (KPIs) or metrics that will be used to measure progress toward the goal. For each indicator, provide a brief description.

Indicator	Description	Current Value	Target Value	Measurement Method	Frequency of Measurement
e.g., Student Engagement Level	*Detail what the indicator measures and any relevant details.*	*Provide the baseline or current value for this indicator.*	*Specify the desired target value or level for this indicator.*	*Describe how you will measure this indicator; e.g., surveys, test scores, usage statistics.*	*State how often you will measure this indicator; e.g., weekly, monthly, per semester.*

Repeat the above for as many indicators as needed.

Data Collection and Analysis:

Tools and Resources:

List any tools, software, or resources required for collecting and analyzing the data related to the indicators.

Responsible Individuals/Teams:

Identify who is responsible for data collection and analysis.

Review and Adjustment:

(continued)

FIGURE 2.2 (*continued*)

Goal Measurement Tracker

Review Dates:

Adjustment Plans:

Outline any plans or strategies for adjusting the approach if the target values are not being met.

Additional Notes:

Include any other relevant information, such as challenges, opportunities, or contingencies related to tracking the goal's progress.

progress and allows for data-driven decision making. Keep this document accessible and ensure regular reviews and updates to track the success of your AI integration effectively.

Achievable

Ensure that the goal is attainable with your school's current resources, skills, and time constraints. Consider what resources or support you might need to achieve this goal and whether it's realistic. For instance, confirm that the AI tool you plan to use is accessible, that you have or can obtain the necessary technology, and that you and your students have the skills or training to use it effectively.

The achievability assessment form (see Figure 2.3) is a practical tool to ensure that each goal is not only envisioned but also meticulously planned and prepared for. By breaking down goals into actionable steps and listing required resources and potential challenges, this form helps create a clear road map for achieving each AI integration objective. Regularly review and update this document as you progress toward your goal to ensure ongoing alignment and adaptability.

FIGURE 2.3

Achievability Assessment Form

Objective Title:

Date:

Prepared by:

Goal Overview:

Brief Description:

Actionable Steps:

Step Number	Description	Expanded Outcome	Persons Responsible	Estimated Completion

Required Resources:

Resource Type	Specific Resource	Current	Required Actions

Potential Challenges and Solutions:

Challenge	Potential Impact	Proposed Solution	Team Responsible

(continued)

FIGURE 2.3 (*continued*)

Achievability Assessment Form

Review and Adjustment:

- Review Dates:
- Adjustment Plans:
- Additional Notes:

Relevant

Your goal should align with broader objectives and your students' specific needs. It should contribute to the overall vision of enhancing learning experiences. Use the relevance checklist in Figure 2.4 to help confirm that the goal makes sense in your context and that it's the right time to pursue that goal. For example, ensure the AI tool addresses a genuine need in enhancing narrative skills or engagement in literature.

Time-Bound

Set a realistic deadline for achieving the goal to foster a sense of urgency and motivate timely progress. Decide by when you expect to see results and plan any milestones along the way. For example, "Implement the AI-driven interactive storytelling tool by the beginning of the fall semester and achieve the target increase in participation by the end of the semester." Figures 2.5 and 2.6 show tools for setting deadlines.

For each of these SMART criteria, using a form or template like those provided here can help clearly articulate, track, and achieve your goals. This structured approach ensures that every objective you set in the context of AI in education is practical, well-planned, and geared toward making a tangible difference in the learning environment. When designing these documents,

FIGURE 2.4

Relevance Checklist

Objective Title:

Date:

Prepared by:

Goal Alignment:

- Objectives: [List the schoolwide or departmental objectives and detail how the goal aligns with each.]
- Student Needs: [Identify specific student needs or challenges the goal addresses and how it aligns with them.]
- Standards: [Note relevant standards or benchmarks and how the goal supports meeting them.]

Stakeholder Buy-In:

- Teachers: [Detail teacher perspectives on the goal and any input or concerns they have.]
- Students: [Summarize student feedback or anticipated reactions to the goal.]
- Parents: [Note parent perspectives or concerns related to the goal.]
- Administrators: [Detail administrative support or concerns regarding the goal.]

Long-Term Impact:

- Sustainability: [Discuss the goal's sustainability and long-term benefits.]

make sure they are user-friendly and adaptable to different goals and contexts. Regularly review and update these goals as you progress, allowing for adaptation as needed. This practical and structured approach can significantly enhance the success and impact of AI integration in your classroom.

FIGURE 2.5

Goal Timeline Template

Objective Title:

Date:

Prepared by:

Overview:

- Brief Description:
- Overall Time Frame: [Start Date] to [End Date]

Milestones:

- Milestone 1: [Description] | [Target Date]
- Milestone 2: [Description] | [Target Date]
- Milestone 3: [Description] | [Target Date]

Checkpoints for Review:

- Checkpoint 1: [Description and Review Date]
- Checkpoint 2: [Description and Review Date]
- Checkpoint 3: [Description and Review Date]

Additional Notes:

Include any other relevant information or contingency plans.

FIGURE 2.6

Example: Goal Timeline

Objective Title: Integrate AI-Based Personalized Learning in 10th Grade Math

Date: June 1, 2024

Prepared by: Jane Doe, Math Department Head

Overview:

- Brief Description: Integrate an AI-based adaptive learning system to provide personalized instruction and practice for quadratic equations, targeting improved understanding and problem-solving skills for all 10th grade Algebra II students.
- Overall Time Frame: September 1, 2024 to May 1, 2025

Milestones:

- Milestone 1: Complete teacher training on AI integration | September 1, 2024
- Milestone 2: Full integration of AI learning in 50% of classes | October 15, 2024
- Milestone 3: Review and adjust AI learning strategies | December 15, 2024

Checkpoints for Review:

- Checkpoint 1: Evaluate initial teacher feedback and student engagement | September 30, 2024
- Checkpoint 2: Midterm assessment of student progress and system effectiveness | October 30, 2024
- Checkpoint 3: Final review of year-end outcomes and planning for next year | December 15, 2024

Additional Notes:

- The timeline may be adjusted based on feedback and progress. Continued professional development sessions are planned throughout the year.

Align Goals with Your Needs

With your goals clearly defined, the next crucial step is to ensure that they align with your students' specific needs and your classroom's capabilities. This alignment is pivotal because it ensures that the AI tools and strategies you select are not merely advanced in terms of technology but also aptly suited and effective for your unique context. Here's an expanded approach to ensuring this alignment:

1. **Assess Technological Infrastructure**
   - Current State: Evaluate the existing technological infrastructure in your school or classroom. Consider the hardware, software, network capacity, and support systems available.
   - Requirements: Determine the technological requirements of the AI applications you're considering. Do they need high-speed internet, specific devices, or any particular software?
   - Gap Analysis: Identify any gaps between what's available and what's needed. Plan for upgrades or look for AI solutions that match your current infrastructure.
2. **Understand Digital Literacy Levels**
   - Students: Gauge your students' digital literacy. What are their comfort levels with technology, and what skills do they need to effectively interact with AI tools?
   - Staff: Assess your teachers' and support staff's digital literacy. Consider professional development needs to ensure that they can effectively implement and use AI in teaching and administrative tasks.
3. **Map AI to Learning Objectives**
   - Curriculum Review: Review the specific learning objectives of your courses and identify where AI can enhance understanding, engagement, or assessment.
   - AI Application Matching: Research AI applications specific to your subject area or instructional needs. Look for case studies or reviews of how similar tools have been used effectively in other settings.

4. **Customize and Adapt**
    - AI Tool Flexibility: Consider how flexible the AI tools are in terms of customization. Can they be tailored to your specific curriculum, teaching style, or students' learning needs?
    - Integration Planning: Plan for the integration of the AI tool(s) you've chosen into your teaching. This might involve piloting the tool in a single course, using it for certain topics, or integrating it across the curriculum.
5. **Ensure Continual Alignment and Feedback**
    - Student Feedback: Regularly gather student feedback on their experience with the AI tools. What do they find helpful or challenging? Use this feedback to make ongoing adjustments.
    - Performance Monitoring: Monitor how the use of AI affects learning outcomes and engagement. Adjust usage based on what is or isn't working.
6. **Address Ethical and Inclusivity Issues**
    - Bias and Accessibility: Be aware of and address any potential biases in AI applications and ensure that all students have equal access to the technology and support they need.
    - Data Privacy: Ensure that any AI tool used complies with data protection regulations and respects the privacy and security of student information.

By taking a comprehensive approach to aligning your AI goals with the needs of your students and the capabilities of your classroom, you can ensure a more thoughtful, effective, and ethical integration of AI into your instruction. This alignment is not a one-time task but an ongoing process of adaptation and refinement, keeping pace with technological advancements and evolving needs.

Attend to Stakeholders

Engaging a broad spectrum of stakeholders is crucial to ensuring the successful integration of AI in education. Each group brings a unique perspective and set of insights that can significantly enrich the planning and implementation process. Here's how you can expand your approach to engaging students, parents, colleagues, and administrators:

1. **Students**
   - Surveys and Forums: Conduct surveys or forums to understand students' familiarity with, and attitude toward, AI. Include questions about their learning preferences and challenges and how they believe AI might help overcome such challenges.
   - Pilot Groups: Invite students to participate in pilot programs with AI tools. Their firsthand experience can provide valuable feedback on the tools' effectiveness, usability, and effect on learning.
2. **Parents**
   - Information Sessions: Hold sessions to inform parents about AI's role and potential in education, addressing any concerns or misconceptions. This is also an opportunity to understand their expectations and apprehensions.
   - Feedback Mechanisms: Establish mechanisms for continuous feedback from parents, such as regular surveys or a section in school newsletters dedicated to AI integration updates and feedback collection.
3. **Colleagues (Teachers and Support Staff)**
   - Professional Development Workshops: Conduct workshops that not only train staff on the technical aspects of AI tools but also facilitate discussions on pedagogical approaches, classroom management, and ethical considerations.
   - Collaborative Planning Sessions: Engage teachers in collaborative planning sessions where they can share ideas on integrating AI into different subjects or activities and provide feedback on proposed AI initiatives.
4. **Administrators**
   - Strategic Meetings: Involve school administrators in strategic meetings to align AI integration with schoolwide goals, policies, and resource allocation. Their support is crucial for facilitating structural changes or investments needed for AI integration.

- Regular Updates and Reports: Provide administrators with regular updates on the progress and impact of AI initiatives. This could include reports on student performance, feedback summaries, and suggestions for future directions.

Engaging a diverse range of stakeholders in the AI integration process is a strategic move that brings several significant advantages. Each group—from students to parents to colleagues to administrators—brings a unique set of experiences and viewpoints regarding AI in education. By gathering these varied perspectives, you gain a holistic understanding of the community's needs, expectations, and apprehensions about integrating AI. Such inclusive involvement is instrumental in identifying potential challenges early. Challenges might range from technical hurdles to resistance within parts of the school community. Recognizing these issues beforehand enables you to plan proactively, crafting strategies that preemptively address these concerns.

Moreover, involving stakeholders directly in the AI integration journey ensures that the initiatives you undertake are not just technically sound but also deeply relevant to your school's needs and ethos. This relevance is crucial in securing a broader buy-in from the community. People are naturally more inclined to support and participate in projects when they have had a say or understand the underpinning rationale.

Additionally, this open engagement fosters transparency, which is essential to build trust. It helps allay fears and clear up any misconceptions about AI, illustrating your commitment to an ethical and student-focused approach to technological integration.

As you interact with these various groups, treat their feedback as more than just valuable input for your immediate planning. View it as an essential resource for continuous refinement and enhancement of your AI integration strategies. Remember, this interaction with stakeholders is not a one-time exercise; it should be a recurring feature of your approach, ensuring that your AI integration is a dynamic, responsive, and inclusive process.

Understand and Apply COPPA and FERPA Regulations

As you introduce AI into your instruction, you must rigorously consider the legal and ethical implications. This includes a thorough understanding and application of related regulations to ensure student privacy and data protection. COPPA, the Children's Online Privacy Protection Act, mandates that you obtain verifiable parental consent before collecting personal information from children under age 13. To comply, you'll need to confirm that any AI tool used in your classroom is COPPA-compliant, securing and maintaining parental consent when necessary. FERPA, the Family Educational Rights and Privacy Act, protects the privacy of student education records. You must ensure that any AI application respects FERPA by allowing parental or eligible student access to their records and not improperly disclosing personally identifiable information.

As you navigate the digital transformation of your classroom with AI tools, your commitment to responsible integration hinges on compliance with legal standards and ethical practices. Your role extends beyond educator to that of a guardian of student privacy and an advocate for ethical digital citizenship, and it should include these actions:

- **Review the AI Tool's Compliance:** Diligently examine AI tools' privacy policies and data practices. It's not enough to accept provider assurances at face value. Investigate whether these tools have undergone audits and conform to COPPA and FERPA guidelines. Check for certifications or endorsements from reputable privacy organizations.
- **Secure Parental Consent:** When personal information is involved, especially for children under 13, make parental consent a priority. Develop clear consent forms that outline what data is collected, how it is used, and who has access. Ensure that the consent process is more than a formality; it should be informative and respect parental authority over their children's data.
- **Be Transparent:** Transparency is nonnegotiable. Establish regular communications with parents and students, clarifying the use of AI tools.

Create a transparent report or dashboard that allows stakeholders to see what data is collected and how it is being used to enhance learning.

- **Protect Data:** You must ensure the integrity and confidentiality of student data. This involves not only secure data storage solutions but also regular training for all staff on data protection best practices. Establish a protocol for responding to data breaches should they occur, including timely notification to affected parties and remedial actions to prevent future incidents.
- **Stay Informed and Compliant:** The landscape of digital law and ethical standards is ever-changing. Commit to ongoing professional development in this area. Attend workshops, enroll in relevant courses, and engage with professional networks focused on educational technology.
- **Educate on Ethical Use:** Embed lessons on digital citizenship within your curriculum. Students should learn about data privacy, the ramifications of their digital footprint, and responsible online interaction. Facilitate discussions on current events related to digital ethics to make the subject matter relevant and engaging.

By following these steps, you fulfill your role as a protector of student privacy in a world of ever-advancing AI. You'll not only comply with the law but also earn your community's trust through ethical practice. This careful approach ensures that the integration of AI into your classroom is both innovative and grounded in a commitment to upholding your students' rights.

Let Your Goals Light Your Path

The goals you've set in this chapter serve as guiding lights, driving your motivation and marking your progress. Keep these objectives in mind, as they remind you that the true purpose of any technological advancement is to support our mission: to educate, empower, and inspire.

Set forth on this path proactively, ensuring that each step aligns with your students' genuine needs and aspirations, thereby transforming the classroom into a dynamic, inclusive, and innovative learning space. As you navigate forward, let your clear vision and the articulated goals direct you. Make these objectives the foundation of your decision making and the measure of your progress. Engage with AI not as a follower trying to keep up with new trends but as a visionary educator shaping the future of learning. Through this journey, aim to not only integrate technology into your teaching but also elevate the entire learning experience, making it more personalized, engaging, and effective for every student. In doing so, you not only embrace the true spirit of education but also realize the potential of AI to further this noble goal within the framework of the HAIL continuum. Your actions will demonstrate how AI can be a powerful ally in the quest to create an educational experience that is more adaptive, inclusive, and inspiring for all.

3

Selecting Appropriate AI Tools

ISTE EDUCATOR STANDARDS

2.3.c: Educators mentor students in safe, legal, and ethical practices with digital tools and content.

2.6.c: Create learning opportunities that challenge students to use a design process and computational thinking to innovate and solve problems.

As you step into the realm of AI integration in your teaching, you face the crucial task of choosing AI tools that align seamlessly with your education goals. Recall the SMART goals you outlined in Chapter 2, crafted with a focus on enriching the learning journey. These goals now serve as your compass, guiding you through the diverse landscape of AI technologies, from adaptive learning systems to real-time analytics and tools that streamline administrative processes. Model the identification and adoption of new digital tools (Standard 2.3.c), demonstrating for students and colleagues alike how to critically select and implement technology that advances learning objectives.

Your objective is to navigate this expanse of options and identify those that resonate most closely with your teaching ambitions. Embark on this selection process by gathering a comprehensive list of AI tools. Challenge students to innovate and solve problems using a design process (Standard 2.6.c), which could involve them in evaluating digital tools and imagining new solutions for their learning challenges. To help you get started, here are some websites and resources that list current AI tools for education:

- *EdTech Magazine* offers a list of innovative AI tools specifically designed for educational purposes. (edtechmagazine.com)
- Common Sense Education provides reviews and ratings of various AI tools and other educational technologies. (commonsense.org)
- ISTE lists and describes various AI tools and resources that educators can use to enhance their teaching. (iste.org)
- EdSurge Product Index is a comprehensive directory of educational technology products, including AI tools. (https://index.edsurge.com)
- Educause is a site that explores new and emerging technologies, including AI tools in education. (educause.edu)
- Artificial Intelligence in Education—SRI International provides a list of AI tools and research on their application in education. (sri.com/artificial-intelligence)

By exploring these resources, you can gather a list of potential AI tools and begin evaluating which ones best fit your goals and your students' needs.

Assess each of these tools against a meticulously crafted checklist that mirrors your SMART goals. In this evaluation, weigh factors such as the tool's relevance to your objectives, user-friendliness, compatibility with your existing technological infrastructure, available support and training resources, and cost-effectiveness. This careful and methodical approach ensures that your choice is not driven merely by the allure of technology but by a clear understanding of how each tool can enhance and elevate the educational experience in your unique classroom environment.

With a shortlist in hand, pilot the most promising tools in your classroom, starting with small-scale implementations to gauge their impact. This trial phase is crucial. Collect feedback from students, observe changes in engagement and learning outcomes, and reflect on your own experience. Using this insightful feedback, make an informed decision about the tool's broader adoption, adjustment, or possible replacement.

As you decide on a tool, plan meticulously for its full integration. Map out how it will weave into your lesson plans, the necessary adjustments to your teaching methods, and strategies for student introduction. Set a timeline with checkpoints to review the tool's ongoing effectiveness and adapt as needed. Remember, the realm of AI in education is dynamic; stay abreast of new developments, continuously seek feedback, and be ready for iterative enhancements to your AI integration strategy. This approach not only underscores the importance of agility in a rapidly evolving digital landscape but also reflects a commitment to ongoing professional growth and the empowerment of students as co-designers of their educational journey.

The aim is clear: You should not merely follow trends but thoughtfully incorporate AI in ways that profoundly enrich the educational experience. Your journey with AI is a testament to the balance between embracing cutting-edge tools and staying true to the core mission of education—fostering an engaging, inclusive, and insightful learning environment.

As you navigate the selection and integration of AI tools into your instruction, consider where each tool sits within the HAIL continuum. As we've discussed, this continuum ranges from humanizing the learning experience to leveraging AI's full capabilities, with augmenting and integrating resting in between. Your task is to not only discern which AI tools align with your goals but also determine the level and manner of AI incorporation that is most beneficial for your classroom.

Begin by reflecting on the HAIL continuum and its implications for your teaching:

Humanize: At this end of the spectrum, focus on tools that emphasize and enhance the human elements of teaching and learning. Ask yourself how a potential AI tool will support emotional intelligence, foster empathy, or enhance creative expression. Tools that allow for personalized feedback or that help identify students' emotional and learning needs are particularly valuable here. Your goal is to ensure that technology amplifies the human connection rather than diminishes it.

Augment: In the middle of the spectrum, seek out AI tools that augment your teaching capabilities. Consider how technology can enhance what you are already doing in the classroom. This might involve using AI to provide insights into student performance, offer real-time analytics, or automate administrative tasks that free you to spend more time on direct student interaction and personalized teaching.

Integrate: Further along the continuum, look for opportunities to integrate AI seamlessly into your curriculum. This involves choosing tools that complement and enhance your teaching methods and learning objectives. Consider tools that adapt to individual learning styles or that can offer differentiated paths through the curriculum.

Leverage: At the far end of the HAIL continuum, consider how you might leverage AI to transform learning experiences. This involves adopting sophisticated AI tools that offer deep personalization, predictive analytics, or the creation of entirely new types of learning experiences. At this level, AI is not just a tool but a partner in designing the future of education in your classroom.

As you evaluate each AI tool, consider where it falls on the HAIL continuum and how that aligns with your classroom's needs and your comfort level with technology. No single spot on the continuum is right for every teacher or every classroom; the key is to find the balance that works for you and your students. Some teachers might prefer to start at the Humanize end, slowly integrating more AI as they become comfortable, whereas others might be ready to jump in at the Leverage end, transforming their classrooms with advanced AI tools from the get-go.

Remember, the HAIL continuum is not just a tool for selecting AI applications; it's a framework for thinking about how you integrate technology into your teaching. It encourages you to be intentional and reflective about the role of AI in your classroom, ensuring that whatever technology you adopt serves the goal of enhancing learning and teaching. As you progress through this journey, continue to reflect on and adjust your position on the HAIL continuum, striving for the most effective, empathetic, and empowering use of AI in your instruction.

Align Tools to Ensure They Work in Your Classroom Ecosystem

As you approach the integration of AI into your classroom, it is vital to conduct a holistic assessment of how each tool will interplay with the unique ecosystem of your classroom. This analysis should extend beyond the immediate allure of innovative features to encompass a broader evaluation of technological, pedagogical, and infrastructural compatibility. Take time to contemplate the following expanded and practical considerations.

Technological Infrastructure Compatibility

Before diving into the exciting potential of AI in your classroom, consider the current state of your technological infrastructure. This crucial step ensures that the AI tools you choose can be smoothly integrated without encountering technical issues that might disrupt teaching and learning processes.

Commence with an exhaustive assessment of your existing hardware and software. This inventory should detail the capabilities of each device, such as tablets and laptops, including their operating systems and specifications like memory and processing power. With this knowledge, you can determine whether the AI tools you're interested in are compatible with your current setup or if your infrastructure requires upgrades.

Moreover, the integration of new AI tools into your established digital ecosystem must be seamless. Evaluate how well prospective AI applications synchronize with your current learning management systems (LMS), student information systems (SIS), and other education platforms. This integration is pivotal for creating a unified user experience where data and resources can be easily accessed across different platforms, which is vital for efficient classroom management. Pay special attention to the application programming interfaces (APIs), plugins, and interoperability options available with the AI tools, along with the technical support offered for integrating these systems.

A thorough examination of both the hardware's capacity and the software's compatibility is essential for informed decision making aligned with the HAIL model. This due diligence helps humanize your approach by using technology familiar to students, augment your resources with AI's advanced capabilities, integrate AI tools into everyday classroom activities smoothly, and leverage your existing technological assets to their fullest potential.

In this context, the insights from Alasadi and Baiz (2023) are particularly pertinent. Their research into generative AI in education underscores the importance of ensuring that AI tools are not only pedagogically valuable but also practically viable within the existing technological frameworks. By incorporating their findings into your evaluation process, you can navigate the complexities of AI integration with confidence, ensuring that your educational technology infrastructure is both robust and ready for the future of AI-enhanced learning.

Digital Literacy and Training Needs

As you contemplate incorporating AI tools into your teaching repertoire, it's essential to consider your classroom's digital literacy landscape. Reflect on the diversity of the students before you, each with their unique digital background. Some may navigate digital spaces with ease, yet others may still be acclimating to the digital world. Your task is to critically evaluate your students' digital literacy. Ask yourself: *Are the AI tools under consideration within the realm of their understanding? Will these tools enhance their learning, or will they present hurdles that might impede their educational journey?*

Choose AI tools that resonate with your students' collective comfort and skill level. If disparities in digital literacy exist, consider incorporating training sessions tailored to bridge these gaps. These sessions could be integrated into the curriculum as a foundational step, ensuring that all students are equipped to leverage the benefits of AI in their learning. This approach not only empowers students but also fosters an inclusive learning environment where technology acts as a bridge rather than a barrier.

Turning to your colleagues and yourself, reflect on the learning curve associated with the AI tool. Each new technology comes with its nuances and complexities. Some tools might be intuitive, requiring minimal training, whereas others might demand a more substantial investment in learning. It's crucial to assess the time and resources available for staff training. Inquire whether the providers of these AI tools offer professional development or training support.

Engaging in such training programs should be feasible within your school's schedule and budget constraints. Consider advocating for time and resources to be allocated toward this professional development, emphasizing the long-term benefits it holds for enhancing the educational experience. Remember, the aim is to integrate AI tools that serve as catalysts for learning, enriching the experience without adding undue complexity or stress. As you embark on this journey, maintain a reflective and analytical mindset, continuously adapting your approach based on feedback and evolving needs.

Pedagogical Alignment

When integrating AI tools into your curriculum, it's critical to ensure they support your core teaching objectives. Pedagogical alignment means selecting and implementing AI technologies that enhance your instructional strategies and learning goals, rather than simply using tech for its own sake. This process requires careful consideration of how each AI tool fits into your overall teaching philosophy and curriculum design.

Begin by revisiting your learning objectives. Ask yourself: How can this AI tool help students better achieve these goals? For instance, if your aim is to improve critical thinking skills, look for AI tools that encourage problem-solving and analysis, not just those that provide quick answers. Consider also how AI can support various teaching methods you already employ. If you value collaborative learning, seek out AI tools that facilitate group work and shared problem solving. For project-based learning, AI could help in research, data analysis, or creative content generation.

Remember, the goal is to use AI as a means to amplify your teaching effectiveness, not to replace your role or fundamentally alter your pedagogical approach. Each AI tool should serve a clear purpose in your instructional design, complementing and extending your teaching practices rather than dictating them.

For instance, if your objective is to enhance collaborative problem solving, an AI tool that facilitates group brainstorming sessions or offers real-time feedback might be particularly effective. On the other hand, if fostering individualized learning paths is your goal, look toward AI tools that adapt to each student's pace and style of learning. Remember, the purpose of technology in education is to amplify the learning experience, making it more engaging, efficient, and tailored to individual needs.

In the diverse landscape of education methodologies, from the interactive dynamics of project-based learning to the reflective solitude of independent research, the AI tools you incorporate must offer the flexibility to adapt. They should be versatile, enhancing various teaching styles and subject matters. Whether you are guiding students through a flipped classroom, orchestrating a symphony of inquiry in a traditional lecture, or navigating the exploratory realms of a project-based setup, the technology should mold to your pedagogical approach.

This means looking for AI tools that offer a range of functionalities that are customizable to different teaching and learning scenarios. For a lecture, an AI tool that aids in creating dynamic presentations or interactive polls might be beneficial. For project-based learning, tools that facilitate collaboration and creative expression, such as digital storytelling platforms or online design labs, may be more appropriate. The key is to select tools that do not impose a rigid structure but enhance and adapt to the organic flow of your teaching.

As you align AI tools with your teaching philosophy and curriculum goals, continuously engage in reflective practice. Observe how these tools influence learning outcomes, seek feedback from students and peers, and be willing to adjust your approach.

Promote Engagement and Interactivity

In the dynamic landscape of education, engagement and interactivity play crucial roles in shaping meaningful learning experiences. As you weave AI tools into your instruction, it's essential to consider how these technologies will invigorate the classroom environment, fostering a vibrant culture of learning. Let's explore the facets of engagement and interactivity that AI tools can enhance.

The heart of any education experience is the student's active participation and interest. As you evaluate AI tools, consider how they will spark curiosity, sustain attention, and encourage active participation. Tools that promote interaction, whether through collaborative projects, interactive simulations, or competitive gamification, can transform the learning experience from passive reception to active exploration.

For instance, AI tools that allow for real-time interaction with content, such as virtual reality simulations or interactive storytelling, can provide immersive learning experiences that are both engaging and memorable. Similarly, tools that facilitate collaboration, such as shared digital workspaces or communication platforms, encourage students to work together, share ideas, and learn from one another.

Moreover, consider the motivational aspects of gamification. Tools that incorporate elements of game design, such as point scoring, competition, or progress tracking, can motivate students by making learning more like a game. These elements tap into students' intrinsic motivation, making the challenge of learning new content exciting and enjoyable.

Feedback is a cornerstone of effective learning, providing students with insights into their progress and guiding them toward improvement. As you assess AI tools, evaluate their capability to deliver timely and personalized feedback. Tools that can provide immediate feedback help students understand their mistakes and learn from them in real time, promoting a growth mindset and an iterative approach to learning.

Look for AI tools that can analyze student responses, identify patterns, and provide tailored feedback that addresses individual needs. Some tools might offer corrective suggestions, alternative approaches, or additional resources tailored to each student's performance. This level of personalization ensures that feedback is not only informative but also relevant and actionable.

On the teacher's side, AI tools can provide valuable insights into student performance, highlighting areas where students excel or struggle.

This information can inform your teaching strategy, allowing you to target interventions more effectively and tailor your instruction to meet your students' varied needs.

In considering both student engagement and feedback mechanisms, look for AI tools that not only captivate and motivate students but also provide them with the support and guidance they need to succeed. These tools should not replace the human element of teaching but rather enhance it, creating a more interactive, responsive, and personalized learning environment. As you integrate these tools into your classroom, remain attentive to their impact on student learning, continually seeking ways to optimize engagement and interactivity for all learners.

Engage in Reflective Dialogue with Peers and Stakeholders

In the collaborative ecosystem of education, the collective wisdom of your peers and the broader community can be invaluable in guiding your selection and implementation of AI tools. Let's delve into how leveraging peer insights and stakeholder input can enrich this process.

Your colleagues, both within your school building and in the wider education community (ask your professional learning network), are a treasure trove of insights and experiences. Engage them, especially those who might have already integrated similar technologies into their teaching, in discussions about potential AI tools. These conversations can illuminate the practical aspects of using AI in the classroom, from overcoming technical challenges to enhancing pedagogical strategies.

Seek out educators who have used the tools you're considering. Ask them about their experiences. What worked well? What limitations did they encounter? How did students respond? This firsthand knowledge can provide a nuanced understanding of the tool's effectiveness and suitability for your context. Additionally, discussions with colleagues who are proficient in educational technology can reveal new possibilities and considerations, helping you make more informed decisions.

Remember, these interactions are not just about gathering information; they're also opportunities to build a supportive community of practice. By sharing experiences and strategies, you and your colleagues can collectively navigate the evolving landscape of AI in education, learning from one another's successes and setbacks.

Beyond your immediate circle of colleagues, consider the perspectives of all stakeholders involved in the education process. This includes parents, administrators, and even students themselves. Each group has unique insights and concerns that are crucial to consider as you integrate AI tools into your teaching. Parents and guardians, for instance, may have questions about data privacy, the impact of screen time, or how AI might change the learning experience for their children. Addressing these concerns openly and providing clear, accessible information can foster trust and support for the integration of new technologies.

Administrators play a key role in the adoption of AI tools because they often make decisions regarding funding, training, and schoolwide policies. Engage them in the conversation early on, presenting the benefits and practical considerations of the AI tools you're considering. Their support can be instrumental in implementing these technologies smoothly and effectively.

Perhaps most important, consider the perspectives of the students who will be using these AI tools. Involve them in the conversation, asking for their input and feedback. After all, they are the primary users of these technologies, and their insights can be incredibly valuable in understanding how AI can enhance their learning experience.

In engaging with all these stakeholders, aim for open, ongoing dialogue. This will not only help in selecting and implementing AI tools that are broadly accepted and effective but also foster a sense of shared ownership and commitment to the success of these technological initiatives. By tapping into the collective wisdom and perspectives of your entire community, you can ensure that the integration of AI into your classroom is thoughtful, inclusive, and ultimately successful.

Ensure Long-Term Sustainability and Support

Under the vital umbrella of long-term sustainability and support, the focus shifts to ensuring that the AI tools you integrate today will continue to serve your objectives effectively in the future. This includes a thorough examination of the vendor support available and a realistic assessment of the cost and budget implications.

The ongoing support provided by the vendor of your chosen AI tool is a cornerstone of its long-term viability. As you evaluate potential tools, delve into the quality and responsiveness of the vendor's customer service. Responsive support can significantly mitigate the challenges of integrating and maintaining new technology in your classroom. Determine the types of support offered—be it live customer service, online resources, or community forums—and consider how accessible and helpful these resources are.

In addition to immediate support, examine the vendor's commitment to continuous improvement through regular updates. These updates should not only fix any bugs and improve functionality but also adapt to the evolving landscape, incorporating the latest research and technological advancements. A vendor that actively updates and improves its product is one that's invested in your long-term success.

The financial investment in AI tools must be weighed carefully against the expected benefits. Begin by understanding the full spectrum of costs associated with the tool, which may include initial purchase or subscription fees, ongoing maintenance costs, and any necessary training or additional equipment. Then consider these costs in the context of your available budget and the tool's expected lifespan.

The return on investment is a crucial factor in this equation. Reflect on how the tool will enhance learning outcomes, streamline administrative tasks, or improve student engagement. The value it brings should justify the investment—not just in monetary terms but also in its contribution to the experience. Some vendors may offer special pricing, grants, or discounts for education institutions, so be sure to explore all available options to make the most of your resources.

In considering both vendor support and cost implications, you're aiming for a balanced approach that secures the long-term sustainability and effectiveness of your AI tools. By ensuring robust support and a viable financial plan, you can confidently integrate technology that will continue to enrich your teaching and your students' learning for years to come.

As you engage in this comprehensive evaluation, remember that adopting AI in your classroom is about thoughtful adaptation rather than mere adoption. It's about finding tools that resonate with your philosophy and enhance the learning experience in meaningful ways. By combining a detailed assessment of each tool's impact on classroom dynamics with a reflective dialogue among peers and stakeholders, you'll illuminate your path forward, ensuring that the technology you integrate into your teaching serves as a bridge to enhanced learning rather than a barrier. This thoughtful approach will help you avoid pitfalls, capitalize on opportunities, and make the most of AI in your instruction.

Two Tools: The Evaluation Checklist and the Compatibility Matrix

In your pursuit to select AI tools that will redefine your classroom, it is imperative to consider their placement within the HAIL continuum. This ensures a balanced integration of technology with the indispensable human aspect of education. To aid this process, two instrumental resources have been developed: the AI tool evaluation checklist (Figure 3.1) and the compatibility matrix (Figure 3.2). The evaluation checklist is designed to scrutinize AI tools through the lens of the HAIL model, emphasizing those that not only enhance the educational experience but also preserve a human-centric approach. On the other hand, the compatibility matrix serves as a navigational aid, aligning your objectives with AI features that effectively augment and integrate into your curriculum. Using these resources allows you to confidently select AI tools that cater to your current needs and embody the HAIL philosophy, fostering a dynamic and forward-looking learning environment.

As you navigate this selection process, keep in mind that the most sophisticated tool is not necessarily the best one for your classroom. The best tool is the one that fits elegantly into your unique narrative, enhancing learning experiences and outcomes.

FIGURE 3.1

AI Tool Evaluation Checklist

When considering AI tools for classroom use, go through the following checklist to ensure a comprehensive evaluation.

1. **Goals Alignment**
   a. Does the tool align with curriculum standards and learning objectives?
   b. How does the tool fit within the HAIL model, particularly in terms of humanizing the learning experience?
   c. Can it be integrated into the existing lesson plans?
2. **Ease of Use**
   a. Is the user interface intuitive for both educators and students?
   b. Are there tutorials and customer support available?
   c. What is the learning curve associated with the tool?
3. **Effectiveness**
   a. Does the tool effectively integrate into the classroom, enhancing student engagement and participation?
   b. What credible evidence or case studies exist that show the tool's effectiveness in leveraging AI for improved learning outcomes?
4. **Data Privacy and Security**
   a. Does the tool comply with student privacy laws (e.g., FERPA, COPPA)?
   b. What data is collected, and how is it used and stored?

5. **Cost**
   a. Is the pricing model sustainable for your budget?
   b. Are there hidden costs such as add-ons or premium features?
6. **Accessibility**
   a. Is the tool accessible to all students, including those with disabilities?
   b. Does it support multiple languages or learning modalities?
7. **Technical Requirements**
   a. What are the hardware and software requirements?
   b. Is it compatible with the school's existing technology infrastructure?
8. **Scalability**
   a. Can the tool be easily scaled to accommodate more users or different contexts?
   b. How does the tool handle data from a growing number of students?
9. **Interoperability**
   a. Can the tool seamlessly integrate with other platforms and tools used in the classroom?
   b. Does it support standard data export and import formats?
10. **Vendor Support and Community**
    a. Is there a strong support community or network for this tool?
    b. Does the vendor provide timely and helpful customer service?
11. **Feedback and Reporting**
    a. Does the tool offer analytics and reporting capabilities to track student progress?
    b. Can educators provide feedback to the vendor for tool improvement?

FIGURE 3.2

Compatibility Matrix

Within the context of the HAIL model, this compatibility matrix is designed to help you align your instructional strategies with the most suitable AI tools, thereby facilitating a seamless integration of technology that enhances, rather than replaces, the human element of teaching.

Teaching Objectives	Tool Feature Required	Example AI Tools
Enhance literacy skills	Interactive reading platforms	• myON • Newsela
Improve math proficiency	Adaptive learning programs	• DreamBox • Prodigy
Develop coding skills	Code practice environments	• Code.org • Scratch
Support language learning	Language learning applications	• Duolingo • Babbel
Facilitate science education	Virtual lab simulations	• Labster • PhET Interactive Simulations
Promote creative writing	Writing assistance tools	• Grammarly • Hemingway Editor
Encourage collaboration	Group project platforms	• Padlet • Google Classroom
Assess student understanding	AI-based assessment systems	• Kahoot! • Quizizz
Personalize learning	Adaptive learning systems	• Smart Sparrow • Knewton
Engage in global awareness	Interactive geography tools	• Google Earth Education • National Geographic Kids

Continuing the Journey

As you conclude this chapter, take a moment to reflect on where we have been. Integrating AI into your instruction is a significant effort filled with both potential and promise. You are not just adopting new technology; you're creating a transformative education experience. With the insights and tools provided, you're now ready to navigate the complexities of AI with confidence and clarity.

Your decisions on AI tools should align with your teaching philosophy and meet the specific needs of your students. The HAIL model guides you through this process, helping you humanize, augment, integrate, and leverage technology in ways that enhance learning. Each step forward is an opportunity to improve your teaching and deepen student engagement, making education more accessible and inspiring.

As you move forward, maintain a reflective approach by continually evaluating the impact of these tools on both your students and your teaching practice. Embrace successes, learn from challenges, and stay connected with your community of peers, students, and stakeholders. Be open to adapting your methods as new insights and technologies emerge.

Your work with AI is a commitment to staying current with advancements while ensuring these tools serve the mission of education. Let your passion for teaching and dedication to your students guide you. The process may be complex and ever-changing, but with a clear vision and thoughtful approach, you will navigate it successfully, shaping a future where education is transformed by the responsible integration of AI.

4

Planning and Designing Activities

ISTE EDUCATOR STANDARDS

2.6.b: Manage the use of technology and student learning strategies in digital platforms, virtual environments, hands-on makerspaces, and in the field.

2.6.d: Model and nurture creativity and creative expression to communicate ideas, knowledge, or connections.

As you start this chapter, you're at a critical point in integrating AI into your teaching. The concepts and strategies you've explored in earlier chapters now come into play as you begin implementing AI in your lesson plans. This chapter focuses on the practical aspects of using AI in the classroom, ensuring each activity aligns with your education goals and meets your students' unique needs.

At this stage, teachers can nurture creativity and creative expression through technology (Standard 2.6.d) by designing activities that allow students to explore and create with AI tools. Whether they're composing music with an AI-assisted app or designing art with a neural network, these experiences can expand their understanding of creativity in the digital age.

While implementing AI in your teaching, it's important to manage student learning strategies in digital platforms and makerspaces (Standard 2.6.b). Create an environment where students can experiment, learn from their experiences, and refine their understanding using AI technologies.

In this chapter, you'll find practical tools and strategies for using AI in education. These include step-by-step instructions for designing lesson plans that meet curriculum standards and incorporate AI effectively. The content encourages critical thinking about how AI can enhance your teaching. You'll also receive practical advice on assessing your resources, understanding your students' needs, and setting achievable goals for AI integration. This chapter addresses common challenges, such as differing levels of technology access and the complexity of some AI tools, and offers strategies to overcome them.

The previous chapters have laid the groundwork for this point. From understanding your classroom in Chapter 1, setting goals in Chapter 2, and selecting AI tools in Chapter 3, you are now ready to design AI-integrated lesson plans. This chapter provides a detailed guide to developing lessons, starting with identifying clear, measurable learning objectives that align with your curriculum.

As you create your lessons, consider AI tools that align with your goals. For example, ChatGPT can help students draft essays and provide personalized feedback, and Copilot can assist with programming assignments by offering real-time guidance and debugging tips. These tools can make learning more interactive and tailored to individual student needs.

AI offers the ability to analyze vast amounts of data on students' learning styles, preferences, and performance, enabling you to craft individualized learning experiences that cater to each student's unique needs and pace. Imagine a classroom where every student's educational journey is finely tuned to their capabilities and goals—where no one is left behind and everyone is challenged just right.

The heart of this chapter lies in the continuum lesson planning template, a tool that embodies the essence of the HAIL model. It is your canvas for planning a structured yet adaptable framework that lets you dynamically plot your course on the HAIL continuum. This template will enable you to craft lessons that resonate with your students, applying the HAIL elements—Humanize, Augment, Integrate, and Leverage—judiciously to create a learning experience that is both meaningful and impactful.

The Art of Lesson Planning in the AI Era

I believe educators have the opportunity to reshape lesson planning with the introduction of AI. This new era encourages you to create not just lesson plans but also engaging experiences that combine human insight with the capabilities of artificial intelligence.

Start by setting clear objectives, now with the additional perspective of how AI can enhance the achievement of these goals. (I discussed this at length already, but it's important to go back to it.) Can AI offer personalized learning experiences for each student? Might it provide real-time feedback that can guide your teaching moment to moment? When defining your objectives, consider how AI can be employed to deepen understanding, foster engagement, and facilitate the practical application of knowledge.

With your objectives in place, it's time to structure your activities. Integrate AI tools that align with your goals. For instance, if you're aiming to improve writing skills, consider AI-driven language learning platforms that offer students immediate feedback on grammar and style. If fostering collaboration is your aim, look toward AI that supports group learning through shared digital workspaces. This chapter provides you with a rich repository of examples, detailing how various AI tools have been successfully incorporated into activities across different subjects and grade levels.

Anticipating outcomes involves not just foreseeing the endpoint but also understanding how AI can dynamically adapt to students' progress and needs. This facet of planning entails considering the various paths learning might take when AI is involved. How will you adjust if the AI tool accelerates learning beyond expectations—or conversely, if students struggle with the technology?

Dive into the practicality of the templates provided here. They prompt you to consider not just the subject matter but also the specific ways AI can assist in delivering content. For instance, a template might suggest starting with a direct instruction using AI for visual aids, followed by an AI-facilitated group activity, and culminating in an individual assessment using AI analytics to gauge understanding.

When constructing the frameworks for your lesson plans, you're essentially creating the blueprints for how instructional strategies and AI applications can intertwine to meet your teaching objectives. Whether it's employing a scaffolded learning approach that leverages AI to build from basic concepts to complex thinking or a flipped classroom model where AI facilitates initial student exploration, these frameworks are foundational to successful AI integration.

Within these frameworks, we explore strategies that enable AI to be introduced smoothly into your lessons. Practical tips for setting up technology, addressing common technical issues, and guiding students to interact with AI responsibly are all part of this process. It's about embedding AI into the fabric of the learning environment so it enhances the educational journey rather than causing disruptions.

Nguyen's (2023) research highlights the transformative potential of AI in education. As you assimilate these strategies into your practice, you move from merely understanding AI's capabilities to implementing them in ways that are both effective and purposeful. By the conclusion of this chapter, the theoretical aspects of AI in education will have evolved into practical, actionable components of your teaching repertoire. Equipped with this knowledge, you're prepared to foster a learning environment where AI is woven into the very fabric of education. This marks the essence of lesson planning in the AI era—a harmonious blend of time-honored teaching practices with the capabilities of technological innovation.

Introduction to AI Tools

As we delve into planning and designing AI-enhanced activities, it is essential to understand the capabilities of various AI tools available. Large language models (LLMs) are versatile tools capable of supporting a wide range of intellectual tasks. These models function similarly to multipurpose tools, assisting with various activities but performing better in some areas than others.

LLMs have the ability to generate humanlike text, understand and respond to complex queries, and even create visual content based on textual descriptions.

Their applications in education are vast and varied, from assisting with lesson planning to providing real-time feedback on student work. Understanding these capabilities allows you to harness their potential effectively in your classroom.

Understanding LLM Capabilities

Large Language Models (LLMs) like ChatGPT, Claude, and DALL-E are powerful AI tools that can significantly enhance the education experience. These models offer a wide range of capabilities that can support both teachers and students in various aspects of learning. From generating text and providing writing assistance to creating visual content, LLMs can be leveraged to make lessons more engaging, personalized, and effective.

In the following section, I'll share the specific capabilities of these models and how they can be applied. Understanding these capabilities is crucial for educators looking to integrate AI effectively into their teaching practices. Let's dive into the key features of these tools and see how they can be used to support different types of learning tasks and subject areas.

1. **GPT-4 and Claude for Textual Tasks**
   - Writing Assistance: These models can generate ideas, draft essays, and offer suggestions to improve grammar and style. For instance, you can use GPT-4 to help students brainstorm topics for a persuasive essay or Claude to provide detailed feedback on their drafts.
   - Content Generation: LLMs can create content tailored to different reading levels and learning styles, making it easier to differentiate instruction. You can generate multiple versions of reading passages or comprehension questions that cater to your students' diverse needs.
   - Interactive Learning: These tools can facilitate interactive learning sessions where students ask questions and receive instant, detailed responses. This can be particularly useful in subjects such as history or science, where students might need help understanding complex concepts.
2. **DALL-E for Visual Arts and Multimedia Projects**
   - Visual Content Creation: DALL-E can generate images from textual descriptions, which can be used to create engaging visual aids for

lessons. For example, if you're teaching a literature class, you can have DALL-E create illustrations based on scenes from a novel, helping students visualize the text.

- Art Projects: In art classes, students can use DALL-E to explore different artistic styles and create unique pieces. This allows for creativity and experimentation because students can generate art without needing advanced technical skills.
- Multimedia Presentations: Enhance student presentations by integrating images generated by DALL-E. This can make projects more visually appealing and help convey complex ideas more effectively.

Practical Applications in the Classroom

Integrating LLMs into your classroom isn't just about understanding their capabilities; it's also about applying them effectively to enhance the learning experience. This section explores practical, subject-specific ways to incorporate LLMs such as ChatGPT, Claude, and DALL-E into your daily teaching practices. We'll cover applications across key subject areas including literacy, math, science, and social studies, demonstrating how these AI tools can support various aspects of learning—from creative writing to complex problem solving.

By thoughtfully incorporating these tools into your lesson plans, you can create more dynamic, personalized, and engaging learning environments. For instance, in literacy, LLMs can assist with everything from generating creative writing prompts to tailoring reading comprehension questions for different skill levels. In math, they can provide step-by-step problem-solving guidance and create interactive exercises. Science classes can benefit from AI-assisted experiment design and data analysis, and social studies teachers can use LLMs for historical analysis and geography visualization.

As we explore these applications, keep in mind that the goal is to enhance, not replace, traditional teaching methods. These AI tools should complement your expertise, allowing you to focus more on individual students' needs and higher-order thinking skills. The following examples are designed to spark your creativity and provide a starting point for integrating LLMs into your specific classroom context. Remember, the key to successful implementation lies in aligning these tools with your pedagogical goals and your students' unique needs.

1. **Literacy**
   - Creative Writing: Use GPT-4 to generate writing prompts or help students develop their stories. The model can provide feedback on plot development, character creation, and stylistic choices.
   - Reading Comprehension: Claude can assist in creating comprehension questions tailored to different reading levels, making it easier to assess student understanding and provide targeted support.
   - Vocabulary Building: Generate vocabulary lists and usage examples with GPT-4, enhancing students' language skills through contextual learning.
2. **Math**
   - Problem Solving: Use GPT-4 to generate step-by-step solutions to complex math problems. This can help students understand different approaches to solving equations and improve their problem-solving skills.
   - Concept Explanation: Use Claude to explain mathematical concepts in simpler terms, providing additional explanations and examples to support student understanding.
   - Interactive Exercises: Create interactive math exercises with instant feedback using these models, allowing students to practice and improve their skills in real time.
3. **Science**
   - Experiment Design: Use GPT-4 to help students design science experiments. The model can suggest variables to test, potential hypotheses, and methods for recording results.
   - Data Analysis: Claude can assist students in analyzing data from experiments, helping them to interpret their findings and draw meaningful conclusions.
   - Research Projects: Generate research topics and outlines with GPT-4, guiding students through the initial stages of their projects and providing a solid foundation for further exploration.

4. **Social Studies**
    - Historical Analysis: Use GPT-4 to generate timelines, summaries, and analyses of historical events. This can help students understand the context and significance of these events.
    - Discussion Facilitation: Claude can provide background information and discussion points for classroom debates, ensuring that students have a well-rounded understanding of the topics.
    - Geography Projects: DALL-E can create maps and visual representations of geographical data, making it easier for students to grasp spatial relationships and geographical concepts.

By integrating these AI tools into your classroom, you can create a more dynamic, engaging, and personalized learning experience for your students. The versatility of LLMs like GPT-4, Claude, and DALL-E allows you to tailor your teaching to your students' unique needs, providing support and enrichment in ways that were previously unimaginable. As you gain practical experience with these tools, you will become more adept at leveraging their strengths and mitigating their limitations, ultimately enhancing your students' educational outcomes.

Templates and Guidelines for AI-Enhanced Learning

As you embark on integrating AI into your teaching, you'll need flexible frameworks that adapt to your unique classroom needs. The following templates and guidelines are designed to support your AI-augmented classroom, serving not as rigid instructions but as adaptable scaffolds to spark creativity and innovation.

These resources will guide you in selecting AI tools that align with your specific lesson objectives, whether you're aiming to personalize learning, provide adaptive feedback, or enhance collaborative projects. Importantly, they consider diverse learning styles and accessibility needs, ensuring your lesson plans remain inclusive and equitable.

The HAIL continuum lesson planning template (see Figure 4.1) offers a structure to inform your pedagogical decisions. It allows you to apply the

HAIL elements—Humanize, Augment, Integrate, and Leverage—selectively, based on your lesson goals, student needs, and subject matter. Remember, you're not required to use all levels of the HAIL model in every lesson. Instead, you can choose to implement only the levels that best suit your current objectives and comfort with AI integration. For instance, you might decide to focus on Humanize and Augment aspects for one lesson, while you explore all four elements in another.

This flexible approach empowers you to plot your own course along the HAIL continuum, crafting learning experiences that resonate with both your students and your teaching style. The examples that follow demonstrate the HAIL model in action, illustrating how these concepts can be adapted to various contexts. Use them as inspiration to blend human insight with AI capabilities in ways that enrich your unique classroom environment.

FIGURE 4.1

HAIL Continuum Lesson Planning Template

This template helps you weave the HAIL (Humanize, Augment, Integrate, Leverage) model into your lesson planning, especially focusing on altering content, instruction, and assessment.

Step 1: Identify Lesson Topic and Objectives

Topic: *Insert subject-specific topic here*

Standards Alignment: *List applicable standards, such as Common Core State Standards, Next Generation Science Standards, etc.*

Objectives: *Define what students should be able to know or do by the end of the lesson, ensuring objectives are measurable and achievable.*

Step 2: Choose the Starting Point on the HAIL Continuum

Consider students' prior knowledge, technology resources, your teaching style, and lesson complexity. Decide whether to start with Humanize, Augment, Integrate, or Leverage.

Step 3: Tailor Content, Instruction, and Assessment

Content Adaptation:

Humanize: *Use AI to generate relatable, real-world scenarios that connect the topic to students' lives. For example, have ChatGPT create personalized word problems for math that incorporate students' interests.*

Augment: *Employ AI-powered visualization tools to enhance understanding. For instance, use DALL-E to generate custom images illustrating scientific concepts or historical events based on lesson content.*

Integrate: *Incorporate AI-driven education games or simulations that adapt to student responses. For example, use an AI-powered platform like Quizizz to create dynamic quizzes that adjust difficulty based on student performance.*

Leverage: *Use AI platforms to create fully personalized learning experiences. For instance, implement an AI system that analyzes student data to automatically generate individualized lesson plans and learning pathways.*

Instruction Adaptation:

Humanize: *Plan for interactive discussions or hands-on activities.*

Augment: *Use technology like smartboards or tablets to demonstrate problems or concepts.*

Integrate: *Combine traditional teaching with AI tools that provide real-time feedback.*

Leverage: *Implement an AI-based instructional platform for data-driven personalized lessons.*

Assessment Adaptation:

Humanize: *Create assessments that allow for student explanations and presentations.*

Augment: *Design digital quizzes or tests that offer instant feedback.*

Integrate: *Employ AI tools for peer reviews or assessments that complement teacher feedback.*

Leverage: *Adopt advanced AI systems for detailed analysis of student responses.*

Step 4: Reflect and Adjust

After the lesson, review the HAIL approach's effectiveness in achieving the lesson objectives. Consider student engagement and understanding. Make notes on what worked and what didn't, and plan adjustments for future lessons.

Reflection Questions:

- Did the AI tools enhance the learning experience as intended?
- How did students respond to the integration of AI in the lesson?
- What changes can be made to improve the next lesson's effectiveness?

Enhanced Storytelling with AI: Ms. Thompson's 3rd Grade Class

Ms. Thompson, a 3rd grade teacher, notices that her class enjoys storytelling but struggles with identifying story elements in readings. She reads a well-known children's story to the class and facilitates a discussion about the characters (Humanize). She then uses an interactive digital storybook in the next session to help students explore character decisions (Augment). For assessment, she combines oral presentations (Humanize) with an AI-assisted tool (Integrate) that provides feedback on their understanding of story elements. This approach allows Ms. Thompson to dynamically adapt her teaching methods, ensuring an engaging, comprehension-focused literacy experience for her students (see Figure 4.2).

FIGURE 4.2

HAIL Continuum Lesson Plan for 3rd Grade Literacy

Step 1: Identify Lesson Topic and Objectives

Topic: Reading Comprehension—Story Elements (Characters, Setting, Plot)

Common Core Standard: CCSS.ELA-LITERACY.RL.3.3—Describe characters in a story and explain how their actions contribute to the sequence of events.

Objective: Students will be able to identify and describe key story elements in a narrative, understanding how characters, setting, and plot interact to create a cohesive story.

Step 2: Choose the Starting Point on the HAIL Continuum

Assess students' current reading levels, classroom technology availability, and your preferred instructional approach to select an appropriate starting point on the HAIL continuum.

Step 3: Tailor Content, Instruction, and Assessment

Content Adaptation:

Humanize: Begin with a class reading of a popular children's story, encouraging students to discuss and relate to the characters.

Augment: Use an interactive digital storybook that allows students to explore different story paths based on character choices.
Integrate: Incorporate an AI-driven reading comprehension tool that asks students questions about the story and provides feedback.
Leverage: Implement a comprehensive AI-powered reading platform that adapts to each student's reading level and provides personalized comprehension exercises.

Instruction Adaptation:
Humanize: Facilitate group discussions and role-playing activities based on the story to deepen understanding of the characters and plot.
Augment: Use digital whiteboards for collaborative mapping of the story elements and their interconnections.
Integrate: Blend traditional instruction with interactive quizzes and games powered by AI that reinforce story elements.
Leverage: Rely primarily on an AI-based platform for instruction, offering individualized learning paths and real-time progress tracking.

Assessment Adaptation:
Humanize: Conduct oral presentations where students narrate their understanding of the story elements.
Augment: Use digital tools for students to create visual story maps or timelines, receiving immediate feedback.
Integrate: Apply AI-assisted tools for peer review of story analyses, complemented by teacher feedback.
Leverage: Employ an AI-driven assessment tool that analyzes students' comprehension and provides detailed reports on their understanding of story elements.

Step 4: Reflect and Adjust

After the lesson, evaluate how well the HAIL strategy met the lesson objectives, focusing on student engagement and comprehension. Modify future lesson plans based on these insights and student feedback.

Understanding Fractions with AI: Ms. Johnson's 5th Grade Class

Ms. Johnson, a 5th grade teacher, notes her students' proficiency in basic fractions but a gap in their ability to apply these skills contextually. Opting to transition from Humanize to Augment in her next lesson, she leads with a story involving fractions in cooking. During instruction, she employs an interactive online fraction calculator for demonstrations, and for assessments, she uses a digital learning platform that provides instant feedback, supplemented by her personal review. By using this HAIL-oriented template, she adapts her teaching methods, ensuring an effective, engaging, and standard-aligned learning experience for her students (see Figure 4.3).

FIGURE 4.3

HAIL Continuum Lesson Plan for 5th Grade Math

Step 1: Identify Lesson Topic and Objectives

Topic: Fractions

Common Core Standard: CCSS.MATH.CONTENT.5.NF.A.1—Add and subtract fractions with unlike denominators by replacing given fractions with equivalent fractions in such a way as to produce an equivalent sum or difference of fractions with like denominators.

Objective: Enable students to proficiently add and subtract fractions with unlike denominators, including mixed numbers, and employ these skills in real-world contexts.

Step 2: Choose the Starting Point on the HAIL Continuum

Consider student background, tech availability, teaching style, and the lesson's complexity when selecting your starting point on the HAIL continuum.

Step 3: Tailor Content, Instruction, and Assessment

Content Adaptation:

Humanize: Use AI to generate personalized, real-world scenarios involving fractions. For example, have ChatGPT create individualized word problems about cooking or shopping that incorporate students' interests and cultural backgrounds.

Augment: Employ AI-powered visualization tools to enhance fraction understanding. For instance, use an AI tool such as DALL-E to create custom images that illustrate fraction concepts based on student-provided scenarios.
Integrate: Incorporate AI-driven education games that adapt in real time. For example, use a platform such as DreamBox Learning, which uses AI to adjust the difficulty and style of fraction problems based on each student's performance and learning pace.
Leverage: Implement an AI system that analyzes student performance data to create fully personalized fraction learning pathways. This could involve an AI that identifies specific fraction concepts each student struggles with, generates targeted practice exercises, and adjusts the curriculum in real time to address individual learning needs.

Instruction Adaptation:
Humanize: Encourage group activities with physical fraction manipulatives to solve problems collaboratively.
Augment: Use digital smartboards to showcase interactive fraction problems from renowned educational resources.
Integrate: Blend traditional teaching methods with AI-supported learning tools providing immediate in-class feedback.
Leverage: Rely predominantly on an AI-based instructional platform to deliver tailored, data-driven fraction lessons.

Assessment Adaptation:
Humanize: Conduct paper-based tests or have students present solutions, explaining fraction problems in their words.
Augment: Implement digital quizzes that offer instant feedback, requiring subsequent teacher evaluation.
Integrate: Employ AI-enhanced peer review tools for assignments, complemented by teacher feedback for thorough understanding.
Leverage: Use an advanced AI assessment system that analyzes responses in detail, proposing custom follow-up activities.

Step 4: Reflect and Adjust

After the lesson, evaluate the effectiveness of the selected HAIL approach in meeting the lesson's objectives, along with gauging student engagement and comprehension. Modify upcoming lesson plans based on these reflections and student feedback.

Narrative Mastery with AI: Mr. Lopez's 6th Grade English Class

Mr. Lopez, a 6th grade English teacher, notices his students' fascination with storytelling but also their struggles with narrative structure. He begins with a classroom activity examining a popular narrative to identify key elements and structures (Humanize). Then he transitions to having students write their own stories, incorporating Hemingway Editor during instruction to aid students in refining their writing (Integrate). For assessments, he combines feedback from Grammarly with his own insights to ensure comprehensive narrative skill development (see Figure 4.4).

FIGURE 4.4

HAIL Continuum Lesson Plan for Middle School Literacy

Step 1: Identify Lesson Topic and Objectives

Topic: Narrative Writing

Common Core Standard: CCSS.ELA-LITERACY.W.6.3—Write narratives to develop real or imagined experiences or events using effective technique, relevant descriptive details, and well-structured event sequences.

Objective: Enable students to write compelling and coherent narratives, incorporating various narrative techniques, rich descriptions, and logical event sequences.

Step 2: Choose the Starting Point on the HAIL Continuum

Selection of the HAIL entry point is determined by evaluating students' prior knowledge of narrative writing, the availability of technology, teaching style, and the lesson's complexity.

Step 3: Tailor Content, Instruction, and Assessment

Content Adaptation:

Humanize: Begin with the analysis of classic narratives or personal storytelling to identify elements of engaging narrative writing.

Augment: Introduce digital storytelling tools like Storybird for students to visually organize their narratives.
Integrate: Use AI-driven language tools like Hemingway Editor to assist students in enhancing narrative structure and clarity.
Leverage: Implement AI-driven writing platforms like Writelab (if available) for comprehensive narrative feedback and development.

Instruction Adaptation:
Humanize: Facilitate classroom workshops on character development, settings, and plot through group activities and shared writing experiences.
Augment: Use interactive whiteboard tools for outlining narrative structures and exploring plot progression.
Integrate: Merge traditional instruction with AI-supported tools like Grammarly for immediate grammar and style corrections in narrative writing.
Leverage: Employ an AI-based educational tool like QuillBot for personalized narrative writing activities, adjusting to individual student learning paces and styles.

Assessment Adaptation:
Humanize: Conduct peer-review workshops and discussion sessions, where students can share and critique each other's narratives.
Augment: Use online platforms like Google Docs for story submission, providing instant feedback using built-in commenting and suggestion features.
Integrate: Apply AI-assisted peer-review systems, supplemented with teacher feedback, to offer a comprehensive review of students' narratives.
Leverage: Implement an advanced AI narrative analysis tool, focusing on structure, coherence, and language use, offering tailored improvement suggestions.

Step 4: Reflect and Adjust

After the lesson, assess how well the HAIL strategy met the objectives, considering student engagement and comprehension. Adjust future lesson plans based on these findings and student feedback.

Summarize Historical Events with AI: Mr. Garcia's 6th Grade Social Studies Class

Mr. Garcia, a 6th grade social studies teacher, recognizes his students' interest in ancient cultures but notes a gap in their ability to summarize historical information. He starts with Humanize, leading a storytelling session about life in ancient Egypt. Then, using Augment, he introduces an interactive timeline in the next class. For assessments, he combines a group project (Humanize) with an AI-powered quiz (Integrate) to evaluate their understanding of ancient Egypt. Through this approach, he ensures an engaging, insightful, and standards-aligned social studies experience for his students (see Figure 4.5).

FIGURE 4.5

HAIL Continuum Lesson Plan for Middle School Social Studies

Step 1: Identify Lesson Topic and Objectives

Topic: Ancient Civilizations—Ancient Egypt

Common Core Standard: CCSS.ELA-LITERACY.RH.6-8.2—Determine the central ideas or information of a primary or secondary source; provide an accurate summary of the source distinct from prior knowledge or opinions.

Objective: Students will understand the key aspects of ancient Egyptian civilization, including its government, culture, and technological advancements, and will be able to summarize primary and secondary sources about this civilization accurately.

Step 2: Choose the Starting Point on the HAIL Continuum

Evaluate students' prior knowledge of ancient civilizations, the classroom's technological capabilities, your teaching style, and the complexity of the subject matter to choose a starting point on the HAIL continuum.

Step 3: Tailor Content, Instruction, and Assessment

Content Adaptation:

Humanize: Start with a class discussion on the daily life in ancient Egypt, using storytelling to bring the era to life.

Augment: Introduce an interactive timeline tool that visualizes the major events and developments of ancient Egyptian civilization.

Integrate: Use AI-driven virtual reality experiences to explore ancient Egyptian landmarks and artifacts.

Leverage: Deploy a comprehensive AI-based educational platform that offers personalized learning modules about various aspects of ancient Egyptian society.

Instruction Adaptation:

Humanize: Facilitate group projects where students create posters or models representing different aspects of ancient Egyptian life.

Augment: Use digital media, such as documentaries or online lectures, to provide in-depth insights into ancient Egypt.

Integrate: Combine traditional teaching with AI-powered quizzes and interactive maps that reinforce historical knowledge.

Leverage: Employ an AI-guided instructional approach using platforms that adapt to each student's learning style and pace, focusing on ancient Egyptian history.

Assessment Adaptation:

Humanize: Conduct a class debate or oral presentations where students share their understanding of ancient Egyptian civilization.

Augment: Implement digital projects where students use online tools to create presentations or infographics summarizing their findings on ancient Egypt.

Integrate: Use AI-assisted peer review tools for evaluating students' projects, complemented with teacher feedback.

Leverage: Apply an AI-driven assessment system that analyzes student responses and provides detailed feedback on their historical understanding.

Step 4: Reflect and Adjust

After the lesson, review the effectiveness of the chosen HAIL strategy in achieving the lesson objectives, considering student engagement and understanding. Make necessary adjustments to future lesson plans based on these reflections and student feedback.

Genetics with AI: Ms. Nguyen's High School Biology Class

Ms. Nguyen, a high school biology teacher, recognizes her students' enthusiasm for hands-on activities but sees that they lack a deep understanding of genetic concepts. Moving from Humanize to Integrate, she organizes a DNA extraction lab, using PhET Interactive Simulations for illustrating the process of transcription and translation. For assessment, she combines traditional lab reports with an AI-assisted tool for evaluating students' conceptual understanding, providing a well-rounded perspective on their learning (see Figure 4.6).

FIGURE 4.6

HAIL Continuum Lesson Plan for High School Biology

Step 1: Identify Lesson Topic and Objectives

Topic: Genetics—DNA Structure and Function

NGSS Standard: HS-LS1-1—Construct an explanation based on evidence for how the structure of DNA determines the structure of proteins, which carry out the essential functions of life through systems of specialized cells.

Objective: Students will understand the structure and function of DNA and how it directs the synthesis of proteins. Students will be able to explain the process of protein synthesis and its significance in biological systems.

Step 2: Choose the Starting Point on the HAIL Continuum

Consider the students' familiarity with molecular biology, available technology resources, teaching styles, and lesson complexity to determine the entry point in the HAIL model.

Step 3: Tailor Content, Instruction, and Assessment

Content Adaptation:

Humanize: Start with discussions and case studies on how genetic research has affected medicine and agriculture.

Augment: Introduce 3D molecular modeling tools like Biorender for visualizing DNA structure and protein synthesis.

Integrate: Use AI-driven simulation tools like PhET Interactive Simulations to explore genetic processes interactively.
Leverage: Use a comprehensive AI-based educational platform such as Khan Academy for in-depth genetics study and personalized learning paths.

Instruction Adaptation:
Humanize: Conduct lab experiments demonstrating DNA extraction and protein synthesis, coupled with group discussions to contextualize the impact of genetics.
Augment: Use interactive smartboard lessons with real-time 3D models to explain complex genetic concepts.
Integrate: Blend traditional teaching with AI-supported simulations and virtual labs, allowing students to experiment with genetic manipulation virtually.
Leverage: Shift predominantly to AI-guided instruction using adaptive learning platforms, providing students with custom learning experiences and problem-solving scenarios.

Assessment Adaptation:
Humanize: Employ paper-based tests and lab reports, where students manually outline and explain genetic processes.
Augment: Implement digital assessments with immediate feedback through platforms like Google Classroom or Canvas, enhanced with automated grading tools.
Integrate: Use AI-assisted evaluation tools to analyze students' understanding of genetic concepts, supplemented with teacher insights for a more holistic view.
Leverage: Deploy advanced AI analytics to monitor student performance and understanding, suggesting tailored follow-up activities and topics for deeper exploration.

Step 4: Reflect and Adjust

After the lesson, reflect on the effectiveness of the chosen HAIL strategy in meeting objectives and engaging students. Adjust future science lessons according to these insights and student feedback.

Algebra with AI: Mrs. Lee's 10th Grade Math Class

Mrs. Lee, a 10th grade math teacher, notes that although her students can perform basic algebra, they struggle with applying methods to solve quadratic equations. Starting with Humanize, she introduces real-world problems that lead to quadratic equations. Moving to Augment, she incorporates interactive graphing tools in the next lesson for visual learning. For assessment, she combines traditional written tests (Humanize) with an AI-powered math platform (Leverage) that provides personalized practice and feedback. Using the HAIL model allows Mrs. Lee to dynamically adapt her teaching methods, ensuring a comprehensive, engaging, and standards-aligned math experience for her students, catering to diverse learning styles and enhancing students' understanding of quadratic equations (making mathematics both accessible and relevant; see Figure 4.7).

FIGURE 4.7

HAIL Continuum Lesson Plan for High School Math

Step 1: Identify Lesson Topic and Objectives

Topic: Quadratic Equations

Common Core Standard: HS.A-SSE.B.3—Choose and produce an equivalent form of an expression to reveal and explain properties of the quantity represented by the expression.

Objective: Students will learn to solve quadratic equations by various methods (factoring, graphing, using the quadratic formula), and understand the applications of these methods in different contexts.

Step 2: Choose the Starting Point on the HAIL Continuum

Assess the students' proficiency with algebraic concepts, the availability of technology resources, your teaching style, and the complexity of quadratic equations to determine the most effective entry point on the HAIL continuum.

Step 3: Tailor Content, Instruction, and Assessment

Content Adaptation:

Humanize: Begin with real-world examples that lead to quadratic equations, such as projectile motion or area calculations.

Augment: Use graphing calculators or interactive graphing software to visually represent quadratic equations.

Integrate: Incorporate AI-driven educational apps that provide interactive problem-solving experiences with quadratic equations.

Leverage: Implement a comprehensive AI-powered adaptive learning platform that personalizes practice problems and explains solutions step-by-step.

Instruction Adaptation:

Humanize: Conduct class discussions on the different methods of solving quadratic equations and when to use each.

Augment: Use digital whiteboards to demonstrate problem-solving techniques and allow students to collaborate on solutions.

Integrate: Blend traditional teaching with AI-supported learning tools that offer immediate feedback on problem-solving exercises.

Leverage: Rely predominantly on AI-based instruction, which adapts to individual student learning styles and paces, providing customized lessons on quadratic equations.

Assessment Adaptation:

Humanize: Have students present solutions to quadratic equations, explaining the reasoning behind their chosen method.

Augment: Use digital quizzes with instant feedback for students to practice solving quadratic equations.

Integrate: Employ AI-enhanced peer review tools for homework assignments, complemented by teacher feedback for in-depth understanding.

Leverage: Use advanced AI assessment systems that analyze student responses in detail and suggest targeted follow-up activities.

Step 4: Reflect and Adjust

After the lesson, evaluate the effectiveness of the HAIL strategy in meeting the lesson objectives, along with student engagement and comprehension. Adjust upcoming lesson plans based on these reflections and student feedback.

A Gradual Embrace

As you incorporate AI into your teaching, it's crucial to approach this integration with deliberation and reflection. The path to incorporating AI into your instructional methods is not uniform; it varies with each educator's skills, experiences, and comfort with technology. This gradual approach is the cornerstone of a successful transition into AI-assisted education.

As part of self-assessing how well you are integrating AI, consider your comfort with digital tools and confirm your proficiency with fundamental digital tools, reflecting on these areas:

- **Initial Experimentation:** Assess the introductory phase of testing AI tools in your classroom.
- **Regular Usage:** Identify if there is an AI tool that aligns with your teaching style and is consistently used in your lessons.
- **Responsive Adaptation:** Evaluate whether you are regularly modifying your use of AI tools in response to student feedback.
- **Advanced Integration:** Determine if you are confidently exploring more sophisticated AI applications to further enhance your teaching.

Mr. Lopez, a science teacher, demonstrates a practical approach to gradually incorporating AI into education. His journey began cautiously, starting with a simple AI-powered vocabulary quiz generator. As his comfort grew, he introduced an AI writing assistant to help students refine their lab reports. Later, he implemented an AI-driven data analysis tool for students' experiment results, and he eventually incorporated a machine learning model that predicts chemical reactions, enhancing his lessons on molecular structures.

As you consider your own path to integrating AI in your teaching, remember that it's an ongoing, flexible process. Mr. Lopez's experience illustrates the benefits of a measured approach to adopting AI in education. The goal isn't to hastily replace traditional teaching methods but to find a harmonious blend where AI tools enhance your existing pedagogical strategies. This gradual integration allows you to evolve your teaching practices at a comfortable pace, ensuring that AI complements rather than overwhelms your educational approach.

Reflective Questions for Educator Growth

Reflecting on your progress and experiences is crucial in this evolution. It allows you to gauge your position within the HAIL continuum and identify areas where you can further develop your skills and strategies. The reflective questions that follow are designed to facilitate this introspection. They encourage you to not only consider where you currently stand in terms of AI integration but also envision the next steps in your journey, ensuring that your approach remains both responsive and aligned with the changing needs of your students and the evolving capabilities of AI technology:

- Where do you currently stand on the HAIL continuum in your AI integration process?
- What specific actions can you take to advance on this continuum at a pace that is comfortable for both you and your students?
- When mapping out the HAIL continuum and preparing for AI integration, what potential challenges should you proactively address, and how can you balance technology with traditional teaching methods?

The following list of prompts can help you decode the AI tool landscape and pick the best tool:

- **Lesson Objective:** Clearly state the aim of your lesson.
- **AI Requirements:** Define what you expect the AI tool to achieve in this context.
- **AI Options:** List viable AI tools that meet these criteria.
- **Selection Criteria:** Include key considerations such as user interface, data privacy, cost-effectiveness, and alignment with goals.
- **Choice of AI Tool:** Select the tool that best addresses the lesson's objectives and meets the selection criteria.
- **Justification for Selection:** Provide a rationale for your choice, highlighting the tool's strengths and relevance to your objectives.

In the case of Mrs. Green, an English teacher navigating the vast options of AI tools to support her students' grammar, her methodical selection process led her to a tool that balanced ease of use, data security, and pedagogical value.

This list of prompts can help you maintain the human–AI balance as you choose tools and plan:

- **Lesson Topic:** State the focus of the lesson.
- **Human Interaction:** Outline the planned activities that require personal interaction and discussion.
- **AI Integration:** Detail the AI tools or activities you plan to implement.
- **Feedback Mechanisms:** Describe how you will collect and use student feedback on both the AI and human elements of your lessons.

For example, Mr. Khan's strategy in teaching about the solar system involved using VR technology to captivate students' interest, followed by structured discussions to solidify their understanding through personal engagement. This illustrates a balanced approach where AI complements traditional teaching methods without overshadowing them.

These reflection points can help evaluate how you're maintaining the human–AI balance:

- **Balance Assessment:** Evaluate whether AI tools are enhancing the learning experience without detracting from personal interaction.
- **Student Feedback:** Consider students' reactions to the blend of AI and traditional teaching methods to inform future lesson planning.

Also reflect on ethical and data privacy considerations. Identify the AI tool you plan to use, and do a data policy review of it, examining the tool's approach to data management and privacy. Anticipate any ethical or privacy concerns that may arise, and plan measures to address these concerns in advance.

For instance, Ms. Rivera's cautious adoption of an AI reading assistant involved an in-depth review of its data policies and clear communication with parents and students, ensuring transparent and informed technology use.

These reflective questions can help you consider data and privacy issues:

- **Data Protection:** How will I verify that the AI tools I'm using adhere to stringent data security standards?
- **Open Communication:** What steps will I take to maintain transparency with students, parents, and other stakeholders?
- **Transparent Practices:** Am I cultivating a transparent ecosystem where students and their guardians are aware of the potential data implications of the AI tools in play?

Embracing AI: Transforming Your Teaching Practice

As Chapter 4 draws to a close, I hope you feel equipped with a clear, actionable understanding of how to integrate AI into your teaching practice effectively. You have a suite of tools and strategies that will transform your classroom into a space where AI fosters deeper understanding and engagement.

This chapter has laid out a systematic approach to adopting AI in lessons, illustrating how these technologies can be introduced to students to spark their interest and enhance their learning experience. The aim has been to demonstrate how AI can be a powerful ally in education, enhancing rather than overshadowing the teacher's role.

Now, as you move forward, you possess the insights needed to ensure that AI tools are used to their fullest potential—maximizing student engagement and elevating the learning process. Carry with you the confidence that comes from this chapter's guidance as you continue to design and implement AI-enhanced lessons. Remember, the goal is to make AI work for you and your students, creating a more dynamic, inclusive, and effective learning environment. With the strategies outlined here, you are ready to take on this challenge and make a significant impact on your students' journey.

5

Implementing AI-Enhanced Activities in the Classroom

ISTE EDUCATOR STANDARDS

2.6.a: Foster a culture where students take ownership of their learning goals and outcomes in both independent and group settings.

2.7.b: Use technology to design and implement a variety of formative and summative assessments that accommodate learner needs, provide timely feedback to students, and inform instruction.

With a clear plan in place, you're ready to implement AI in your classroom. This chapter focuses on executing AI-enhanced activities. It covers the use of technology for both formative and summative assessment (Standard 2.7.b), using tools that deliver real-time data on student understanding and allowing you to adapt your teaching to meet students' changing needs.

This chapter will guide you through the steps of conducting these activities, monitoring student engagement, and providing the support necessary to ensure a smooth and successful integration of AI into your teaching. It's important to facilitate a culture where students independently manage their learning goals (Standard 2.6.a), fostering an environment that encourages them to set, reflect on, and achieve their objectives with the support of AI tools.

Initiating AI integration into your classroom is a crucial step that lays the groundwork for successfully adopting and effectively using AI tools. This process begins with a thorough revisit of your lesson plans, ensuring that they seamlessly incorporate the chosen AI tools to amplify the learning experience. To make this process super-practical, consider the following steps, complete with tools and templates.

Preparing an Introduction Session

The introduction session is a cornerstone in setting the tone for AI integration in your classroom. It's crucial to create an environment that demystifies AI, aligns it with goals, and emphasizes its relevance in real-world scenarios. Here's how to expand and structure this session effectively:

- Clearly articulate the value of AI in education, illustrating how it can support individualized learning paths.
- Showcase examples of AI in action, providing case studies or demonstrations that are relevant to the subjects you teach.
- Create interactive demonstrations that allow students to experience AI tools firsthand, fostering familiarity and comfort.
- Discuss the role of AI in modern society, encouraging students to think critically about its application and impact.

By demystifying AI and situating it within the context of both the classroom and the larger world, you pave the way for students to embrace these technologies as a natural and beneficial component of their education. This sets the stage for a classroom environment where AI is not seen as a distant, abstract concept but as a tangible and valuable tool they can leverage in their educational journey.

Setting the Stage

Begin with a brief overview of what AI is and its growing role in various aspects of life, including education. Use simple, relatable examples to explain AI concepts. For instance, you might compare AI algorithms to recipe instructions to illustrate how computers learn to perform tasks. Clearly state the objectives, such as understanding AI basics, learning how to use a specific AI tool, and appreciating its role in enhancing education. Encourage an interactive atmosphere where questions and curiosity are welcomed.

Demonstrating the Tool

Use a projector or smartboard for a live demonstration of the AI tool. Walk through the key features and functionalities step by step. For instance, if you're using an AI language learning app, show how it offers personalized vocabulary exercises. Highlight the tool's user-friendly aspects to alleviate any apprehensions about using technology. Engage students in a hands-on experience with the AI tool during the demonstration. This could be a simple exercise, like entering a sample query or completing a small task using the tool. Consider creating a fun, competitive element, such as a quiz or game, using the AI tool to drive engagement.

To further illustrate the practical applications and integration of advanced AI tools in your classroom, let's explore detailed activities with specific AI tools like GitHub Copilot, Microsoft Copilot, ChatGPT, DALL-E, and Claude. These tools can significantly enhance various aspects of learning and teaching, making your classroom a dynamic and engaging environment.

GitHub Copilot

Objective: To help students learn to code by providing real-time code suggestions and explanations.

- **Introduction:** Begin by explaining the purpose and functionality of GitHub Copilot. Highlight how it can help students write code more efficiently by providing suggestions and autocompleting code.
- **Demonstration:** Use a projector to show GitHub Copilot in action. Open a code editor like Visual Studio Code and demonstrate how Copilot suggests code as you type. Walk through a simple coding exercise, such as creating a basic HTML page or Python script.
- **Hands-On Activity:** Have students open their code editors and write a simple program with the help of Copilot. For example, they can create a basic calculator application in Python, with Copilot assisting them in writing the functions for addition, subtraction, multiplication, and division.

- **Discussion:** After the exercise, facilitate a discussion on how Copilot helped them, what they found useful, and any challenges they encountered. Encourage them to think about how they can use Copilot for future coding projects.

Microsoft Copilot

Objective: To enhance productivity in classroom activities like writing reports, analyzing data, and creating presentations.

- **Introduction:** Explain Microsoft Copilot's functionalities and how it can assist in various Office applications. Highlight its features, such as generating text in Word, creating data visualizations in Excel, and designing slides in PowerPoint.
- **Demonstration:** Show how to use Microsoft Copilot in different Office applications. For example, open a Word document and demonstrate how Copilot can help write a report, or use Excel to show how it can create and analyze data charts.
- **Hands-On Activity:** Assign students a research project where they need to write a report, create data visualizations, and present their findings. Students will use Microsoft Copilot to assist with writing sections of the report, creating data charts, and designing PowerPoint slides.
- **Discussion:** After the project, hold a discussion on how Microsoft Copilot facilitated their work. Ask students to share their experiences and any insights they gained from using the tool.

ChatGPT

Objective: To facilitate writing, brainstorming, and research assistance.

- **Introduction:** Introduce ChatGPT as an AI tool that can assist with generating text, answering questions, and providing research support.
- **Demonstration:** Show how to use ChatGPT to brainstorm ideas for an essay, generate outlines, or get answers to specific questions. Demonstrate a live session where you ask ChatGPT to help outline an essay or write a paragraph on a given topic.

- **Hands-On Activity:** Have students use ChatGPT to brainstorm and outline an essay on a topic of their choice. They can also use it to draft sections of their essay or get answers to research questions.
- **Discussion:** After the activity, discuss how ChatGPT helped in the writing process, any limitations students encountered, and how they can effectively use it for future assignments.

DALL-E

Objective: To inspire creativity and enhance visual projects by generating images from text descriptions.

- **Introduction:** Explain how DALL-E works and its potential applications in creative projects.
- **Demonstration:** Show how to use DALL-E by entering text prompts to generate images. For example, type in "a futuristic cityscape at sunset" and demonstrate the generated images.
- **Hands-On Activity:** Assign students a creative project where they need to use DALL-E to generate images for a story they are writing or for a presentation. Encourage them to experiment with different prompts to see the variety of images DALL-E can produce.
- **Discussion:** After the project, discuss how DALL-E helped in visualizing their ideas. Ask students to share their generated images and how they incorporated them into their projects.

Claude

Objective: To assist with various tasks such as generating text, providing detailed explanations, and supporting interactive learning activities.

- **Interactive Q&A Sessions:** Use Claude to generate detailed answers to student questions during lessons. This can help in providing diverse perspectives and comprehensive explanations on complex topics.
- **Writing Assistance:** Similar to ChatGPT, Claude can aid in writing assignments by suggesting improvements, offering stylistic enhancements, and ensuring grammatical accuracy. Demonstrate this by taking a sample student essay and using Claude to show real-time editing and suggestions.

- **Creative Projects:** Engage students in creative projects by using Claude to brainstorm ideas, create storylines, or develop characters. This can be particularly useful in English and creative writing classes.
- **Research Support:** Use Claude to assist students in gathering information and summarizing research topics. This can streamline the research process and help students focus on critical analysis and synthesis of information.

Integrating Large Language Models in the Classroom

LLMs like GPT-4, Claude, and others are versatile tools capable of supporting a wide range of intellectual tasks. These models function similarly to multipurpose tools, assisting with various activities but performing better in some areas than others. To effectively use these models, you need practical experience—typically around 10 hours—to fully understand their strengths and limitations.

When implementing LLMs, it's crucial to recognize their strengths and limitations. These models are designed to be broadly applicable rather than specialized, akin to interacting with a smart but unpredictable assistant. Using GPT-4 to assist with lesson planning can yield impressive results due to its capability to generate detailed and comprehensive plans that align with standards, incorporate diverse instructional strategies, and offer creative ideas for activities and assessments. GPT-4 can suggest various instructional approaches, recommend resources, and even generate differentiated tasks for students with varying learning needs. However, for simpler and more routine tasks like organizing classroom schedules, more specialized tools might be better suited (Google Calendar, ClassDojo, PowerSchool, and learning management system platforms).

ChatGPT and Claude for Writing Assistance

- **Idea Generation and Feedback:** Use these models to generate ideas and provide feedback on student writing. For example, take a sample essay and demonstrate how the model suggests improvements in style and grammar.

This can be particularly useful in helping students refine their writing skills by providing concrete examples of how to improve their work.

- **Creative Writing Projects:** Integrate these models into creative writing assignments. Students can brainstorm story ideas, develop plots, and receive real-time feedback on their narratives, enhancing their creativity and critical thinking skills. For instance, students could write a short story and use the model to help develop character arcs or plot twists.

DALL-E for Visual Arts

- **Visual Content Creation:** Use DALL-E to generate images that complement lesson plans. For instance, in a literature class, students can describe scenes from a novel and create visual representations. This helps in visualizing and better understanding the text, making the learning experience more immersive.
- **Art Class Applications:** In art classes, students can explore different artistic styles and create unique artworks using DALL-E. This allows for experimentation without needing advanced technical skills, making art more accessible. For example, students can describe a concept or theme, and DALL-E can generate an array of visual interpretations for them to analyze and discuss.

Microsoft Copilot for Productivity

- **Lesson Planning and Administration:** Integrate Microsoft Copilot into lesson planning and administrative tasks. Copilot can draft documents, analyze data, and manage schedules, streamlining your workflow and providing more time for student interaction. For example, you can use Copilot to create detailed lesson plans that align with curriculum standards, complete with timelines and resource lists.
- **Student Organization:** Copilot can help students organize their study schedules, create project plans, and manage group work. This promotes

better time management and collaboration skills. For instance, students can use Copilot to develop a study plan for an upcoming exam, breaking down topics into manageable study sessions and tracking their progress.

Math Problem Solving with ChatGPT and Claude

- **Step-by-Step Solutions:** Use ChatGPT and Claude to help students work through complex math problems by providing step-by-step solutions and explanations. This can be particularly useful for understanding algebraic expressions or calculus problems.
- **Practice Problem Generation:** Create practice problems tailored to different difficulty levels. For example, ask the model to generate quadratic equations for students to solve, providing instant feedback and hints.

DALL-E for Geometry and Visualization

- **Visualizing Geometric Concepts:** Use DALL-E to create visual representations of geometric concepts. For example, students can describe a three-dimensional shape and see it rendered visually, which aids in understanding spatial relationships and properties.
- **Graphical Interpretations:** In statistics or algebra, generate graphs and charts that visually represent data sets or equations. This helps students better grasp abstract concepts through visual learning.

Experiment with these tools within your teaching role. This hands-on approach helps in understanding their practical utility and limitations. It's important to stress that by the time you read this, new LLMs may have emerged. Therefore, focus on the contextual use of these tools in the classroom rather than on the specific names or companies.

By integrating LLMs thoughtfully into your classroom, you can enhance the learning experience, making it more interactive, personalized, and engaging. Whether through writing assistance, visual arts, productivity tools, or math applications, these models offer diverse possibilities to enrich education.

Discussing Purpose and Benefits

When explaining the connection between AI tools and education objectives, it's important to show how these technologies support and enhance course goals. AI tools like ChatGPT create personalized learning paths that adjust to each student's pace and learning style, offering a more customized experience. These tools provide instant feedback, making the learning process more efficient by quickly correcting mistakes and helping students understand the material better.

For instance, AI tools designed for data analysis not only teach students about data manipulation and interpretation but also equip them with skills that are highly valued across numerous industries, including health care, finance, and the creative sectors. This connection between classroom learning and real-world application is vital because it prepares students for the demands of the modern workforce.

Adigüzel, Kaya, and Cansu (2023) delve into the transformative potential of AI tools like ChatGPT, noting its capacity to revolutionize education by providing an interactive, adaptive learning environment. They discuss how integrating such AI tools in the classroom not only supports knowledge acquisition but also fosters the development of critical thinking and problem-solving skills, which are indispensable in various professional fields.

By showcasing real-world examples where AI significantly affects sectors outside education, educators can illustrate the broader relevance and potential career pathways that these competencies enable. For example, in health care, AI-driven data analysis tools are crucial for predictive diagnostics and personalized medicine, whereas in finance, they are used for risk assessment and algorithmic trading. In the creative industries, AI facilitates design, music production, and content creation, showcasing its versatility and the breadth of its applications.

Such examples not only emphasize AI's importance in current and future job markets but also help ground theoretical knowledge in practical, tangible outcomes. This approach underscores the broad significance of AI in education and its capacity to empower students with skills that transcend the classroom, underscoring the study by Adigüzel and colleagues and reaffirming AI's transformative potential in revolutionizing instruction.

Encouraging Curiosity and Experimentation

To effectively encourage curiosity and experimentation among your students regarding AI tools, it's essential to create an atmosphere that fosters inquiry, exploration, and open communication. Here are expanded strategies to achieve this:

1. **Facilitate Thought-Provoking Discussions**
   - Pose Open-Ended Questions: Start discussions with open-ended questions that prompt students to think about the potential impact of AI on their learning and future. For example, ask, "How do you think AI can change the way we learn new subjects?" or "What are some tasks you believe AI could help you with in your studies?"
   - Encourage Speculative Thinking: Invite students to imagine future scenarios or possibilities with AI in education. Questions like "What would a classroom fully integrated with AI look like in 10 years?" can stimulate creative thinking.
2. **Encourage Interactive Exploration of the AI Tool**
   - Guided Exploration: Initially, guide students through the tool's basic features. Once they are comfortable, encourage them to explore more advanced features on their own or in groups.
   - Discovery-Based Learning: Design activities where students learn by discovering features of the AI tool. For instance, assign tasks that require them to use specific functions of the tool, promoting hands-on learning.
3. **Create an Open Environment**
   - Feedback Sessions: Regularly schedule sessions when students can discuss their experiences with the AI tool. Encourage them to share what they like, what challenges they face, and any interesting findings.

- Question-Friendly Atmosphere: Emphasize that all questions are valid and welcome. Consider having a dedicated "question box" or an online forum where students can post their queries and feedback anonymously.

4. **Encourage Collaborative Learning**
   - Group Tasks: Assign group projects where students use the AI tool collaboratively. This can lead to shared learning experiences and peer-to-peer teaching, which can be very effective in understanding technology.
   - Peer Teaching: Encourage students who grasp the AI tool quickly to help their peers who might be struggling. This not only creates a supportive learning environment but also reinforces the knowledge of the students who are teaching.
5. **Integrate AI Tool Exploration into Assignments**
   - Incorporate Tool Exploration in Assignments: Design assignments that require the use of the AI tool, ensuring that students must explore its features to complete the task.
   - Reward Curiosity: Recognize and reward creative uses or discoveries made using the AI tool. This could be through verbal praise, showcasing students' work, or even small rewards.
6. **Use Real-World Scenarios**
   - Case Studies: Use real-world case studies where AI is being used in the field of study. Discuss these in class to illustrate the practical applications of AI.
   - Guest Speakers: Invite professionals who use AI in their work to speak with your students, providing them with real-world insights into the application of AI.

Additional Tips for the Introduction Session

1. **Visual Aids:** Incorporate infographics, videos, or diagrams to make complex AI concepts more understandable.

2. **Feedback Mechanism:** Have a system in place for students to provide feedback or ask questions anonymously, encouraging participation from those who might be hesitant to speak up.
3. **Follow-Up Resources:** Provide supplementary materials after the session, like tutorial videos, FAQs about the AI tool, or links to further reading for students who want to explore more.
4. **Parental/Guardian Involvement:** Consider sending a brief overview of the AI tool and its educational purpose to parents or guardians to keep them informed and engaged in their child's learning process.

As you prepare for the introduction session with AI tools, it's crucial to align this process with the HAIL model. This model will serve as a scaffold, guiding you to create an introduction session that balances human insight with the capabilities of AI.

1. **Humanizing the Introduction:** Begin by humanizing the session. Make sure to connect on a personal level with your students, acknowledging any apprehensions or excitement they might have about using AI in the classroom. Share anecdotes or experiences to create a relatable context for the AI tools.
2. **Augmenting Understanding with AI:** Use the AI tools to augment the students' understanding of the subject matter. For example, if you're introducing an AI language learning app, demonstrate how it can personalize vocabulary learning to each student's pace and style, thereby enhancing their individual learning experience.
3. **Integrating AI into the Lesson Flow:** Discuss with your students how these AI tools will be integrated seamlessly into your regular teaching methods. This might involve showing how an AI simulation will be used alongside traditional teaching to provide a richer understanding of complex concepts.
4. **Leveraging AI for Deeper Insights:** Explain how AI tools can be leveraged for deeper insights into students' learning patterns. For instance, show how AI analytics can help identify areas of strength and areas that need more focus, allowing you to tailor your teaching more effectively to students' needs.

By incorporating the HAIL model in your introduction session, you're setting the stage not only for the effective use of AI tools but also for an educational experience that harmoniously blends technology with the human aspects of teaching. This approach ensures that your classroom remains a dynamic learning environment where technology is used thoughtfully and strategically to enhance education.

Implementing a Specific AI Tool: A Scenario

Let's dive into a scenario that illustrates how to implement a specific AI tool in the classroom. This section will walk you through the process using an AI tool and provide a detailed example you can adapt to your teaching context.

Scenario: Using an AI-powered writing assistant in an English class

Objective: To enhance students' writing skills by integrating an AI-powered writing assistant tool

Step 1: Selecting the AI Tool

- Tool Chosen: Use an AI-powered writing assistant like Grammarly or a similar tool.
- Reason for Selection: This tool can help students improve their writing by providing real-time feedback on grammar, spelling, style, and tone, making it a practical choice for an English class.

Step 2: Preparing the Introduction Session

- Overview: Start with an overview of the tool, explaining its capabilities and how it uses AI to analyze a text and suggest improvements in writing.
- Demonstration: Show a live demo of the tool in action, perhaps by taking a paragraph written by a student (with their permission) and running it through the tool to show the suggested improvements.

Step 3: Interactive Classroom Activity

- Activity Design: Create an activity in which students write a short essay or a paragraph on a given topic.

- Using the Tool: Instruct students to use the AI writing assistant to review and edit their work.
- Collaborative Review: Encourage students to work in pairs or small groups to discuss the feedback provided by the tool and make revisions accordingly.

Step 4: Discussion and Feedback

- Group Discussion: After the activity, lead a discussion on the experience. Ask questions like "How did the AI tool help you improve your writing?" or "Did you disagree with any of the AI suggestions?"
- Individual Feedback: Encourage students to reflect on how the tool affected their writing process and any new insights they gained about their writing style or common mistakes.

Step 5: Integrating into Regular Assignments

- Long-Term Use: Plan to integrate this AI tool into regular writing assignments, encouraging continuous use and familiarization.
- Progress Tracking: Use the tool's analytics (if available) to track improvements in students' writing over time, discussing these trends during feedback sessions.

Step 6: Evaluation and Reflection

- Student Reflections: Periodically ask students to write a short reflection on their experience using the tool and how it has affected their writing skills.
- Teacher Evaluation: Evaluate the effectiveness of the tool in improving students' writing skills based on assignment grades, student feedback, and your observations.

Step 7: Engaging Parents and Guardians

- Communication: Inform parents and guardians about the AI tool being used in the classroom. Explain its benefits and how it's helping improve their child's writing skills.
- Feedback from Parents: Encourage parents to provide feedback based on any changes they observe in their child's writing at home.

Additional Resources

- Supplementary Materials: Provide students with resources on best practices in writing, complementing the AI tool's feedback.
- Professional Development: Consider attending workshops or webinars on effectively integrating AI tools into teaching to continuously enhance your approach.

By following this scenario, you can effectively integrate an AI-powered writing assistant into your English class, providing a hands-on example of how AI can be used to enhance learning outcomes. This approach ensures that students not only learn to use the AI tool but also understand its role in supporting and improving their writing skills.

Conducting AI-Enhanced Activities

The integration of AI into classroom activities marks a significant shift in education practices, offering unprecedented opportunities for personalized learning, data-driven insights, and innovative problem solving. However, the successful implementation of AI-enhanced activities requires more than just introducing new technology; it demands a thoughtful, structured approach that balances technological prowess with pedagogical wisdom. As educators, our role evolves from mere instructors to facilitators of AI-augmented learning experiences, guiding students through this new terrain of digital discovery.

This section delves into the multifaceted process of conducting AI-enhanced activities in your classroom. We'll explore strategies that go beyond basic implementation, focusing on creating an environment where AI tools seamlessly blend with traditional teaching methods to enhance learning outcomes. From meticulous technical preparation to fostering a culture of curiosity and exploration, we'll cover the essential elements that transform AI from a novel classroom addition to an integral part of the learning ecosystem.

Our journey through this section will encompass four key areas: setting up the optimal learning environment, facilitating engaging AI-driven activities, encouraging student exploration and creativity with AI tools, and managing the dynamics of collaborative AI-enhanced projects. By mastering these aspects, you'll be well equipped to navigate the challenges and harness the full potential of AI in education, ensuring that your students adapt to this technology and thrive in an AI-enhanced learning landscape.

Setting Up the Environment

1. **Technical Setup**
    - Preactivity Checklist: Create a checklist to ensure that all technical aspects are covered. This should include checking the functionality of AI software, ensuring that all devices are charged or plugged in, and verifying network connectivity.
    - Troubleshooting Plan: Have a basic troubleshooting plan in place for common technical issues, such as login problems or software glitches. Share this with students or have it displayed in the classroom.
2. **Clear Instructions**
    - Step-by-Step Guides: Develop and distribute step-by-step guides for using the AI tools. These can include screenshots, FAQs, and tips for navigating common challenges.
    - Demo Videos: Consider creating or sourcing short demonstration videos that students can refer to for a visual and auditory explanation of how to use the tools.

Facilitating the Activity

1. **Guided Start**
    - Interactive Walkthrough: Start the activity with an interactive walkthrough of the AI tool. This could involve a live demonstration of its features, followed by a Q&A session to address any immediate queries.
    - Pair and Share: Pair students up and have them explore the initial features of the tool together. This approach can help reduce anxiety and promote peer learning.

2. **Observation**
    - Circulate and Observe: Actively move around the classroom, observing how students interact with the tool. Pay attention to both their screens and their nonverbal cues.
    - Take Notes: Keep a record of your observations, noting down which features students use most, any areas of confusion, and how quickly they adapt to the tool.

Encouraging Exploration

1. **Open Exploration**
    - Challenge Tasks: Set up exploration challenges or scavenger hunts that require students to discover and use different features of the tool.
    - Self-Directed Learning: Allocate time for students to explore the tool at their own pace, encouraging them to delve into areas of personal or academic interest.
2. **Prompt Questions**
    - Inquiry-Based Prompts: Use questions that encourage critical thinking and exploration, such as "How could this feature enhance your learning?" or "How else might you use this tool to complete your task?"

Facilitating Group Dynamics

1. **Group Work**
    - Role Assignment: In group activities, assign specific roles such as navigator, researcher, or presenter to ensure active participation from all group members.
    - Collaborative Projects: Design projects where collaboration is key to success, requiring students to use the AI tool to work together effectively.
2. **Managing Group Dynamics**
    - Observation of Interactions: Monitor how students interact within groups. Intervene if necessary to ensure that all voices are heard and valued.

- Reflection and Feedback: After group activities, conduct a reflection session where students can discuss what worked well in their group dynamics and what could be improved.

By expanding on these methods, you can create a structured yet flexible environment for conducting AI-enhanced activities. This approach not only helps you effectively integrate AI into your teaching but also supports diverse learning styles and encourages active participation from all students.

Monitoring Engagement and Providing Support

Effectively monitoring student engagement and providing appropriate support are crucial for the success of AI-enhanced activities in the classroom. To ensure these elements are addressed thoroughly, it is important to establish clear strategies for observing student interaction with AI tools and providing timely assistance when needed. This involves not only tracking participation levels but also assessing the quality of engagement, such as students' depth of understanding and their ability to apply AI tools to their learning tasks. Additionally, offering differentiated support based on individual student needs can help bridge gaps in understanding and ensure that all students benefit from the integration of AI into the learning environment. Regular check-ins and feedback sessions can further enhance the effectiveness of monitoring and support efforts, creating a responsive and supportive classroom culture.

Assessing Engagement

1. **Detailed Observation of Reactions**
    - Behavioral Indicators: Look for behavioral indicators of engagement, such as students actively asking questions, volunteering to share their work, or showing enthusiasm in using the AI tool.
    - Nonverbal Cues: Pay attention to nonverbal cues. Are students leaning forward, focused on their screens, or showing signs of boredom or confusion?

2. **Using Engagement Tools**
    - Analytics and Reporting: Use any analytics or reporting features the AI tool offers to gain insights into student usage patterns, time spent on tasks, and areas where they struggle.
    - Feedback Mechanisms: Implement feedback mechanisms within the AI tool, such as polls or interactive quizzes, to gauge understanding and engagement levels.

Providing Support

1. **Tailored Assistance for Challenges**
    - Individual Check-Ins: Conduct individual check-ins with students who appear to be struggling. This allows for personalized support and helps identify specific challenges they may be facing.
    - Resource Sharing: Share additional resources, such as tutorials or guides, to assist students who need extra help with the AI tool.
2. **Differentiated Support Strategies**
    - Peer Mentoring: Pair students who are proficient with the tool with those who need more help. This peer-to-peer support can be an effective way to build confidence and skills.
    - Small-Group Sessions: Organize small-group sessions for students who need extra support, focusing on specific features or aspects of the AI tool.

Encouraging Risk-Taking

1. **Creating a Positive Reinforcement Environment**
    - Celebrate Exploration: Regularly acknowledge and celebrate when students try new features or approaches, even if they don't yield perfect results.
    - Showcase Successes and Learnings: Occasionally, showcase students' successful use of the tool or how they overcame challenges, which can motivate others.

2. **Promoting a Safe Learning Environment**
    - Encourage Questions and Mistakes: Create a classroom culture in which questions and mistakes are not only accepted but encouraged as part of the learning process.
    - Reflect and Learn from Errors: After activities, encourage students to reflect on what they learned from any mistakes they made, turning these into valuable learning experiences.

Adapting Your Approach

1. **Maintaining Flexibility in Teaching Methods**
    - Responsive Adjustments: Be ready to adjust your teaching methods or lesson plans based on the ongoing assessment of student engagement and understanding.
    - Dynamic Grouping: Consider regrouping students based on their comfort and proficiency with the AI tool, allowing for more targeted instruction and support.
2. **Gathering and Implementing Continuous Feedback**
    - Regular Feedback Channels: Establish regular channels for students to provide feedback on their experience with the AI tool, either through digital surveys, suggestion boxes, or open discussions.
    - Action on Feedback: Actively use the feedback to make improvements. Communicate back to students how their input has shaped changes in the classroom, reinforcing their role in shaping their learning environment.

By monitoring engagement and providing support in this detailed manner, you create an inclusive, responsive, and dynamic learning environment. This approach not only leverages the power of AI tools but also ensures that these tools are used effectively to cater to your students' diverse learning needs and styles.

Assessment and Feedback

The realm of assessment and feedback is experiencing a significant shift with the introduction of AI. This technological evolution presents educators with novel opportunities to enhance their evaluation methods, offering more detailed, immediate, and individualized insights into student performance. In this section, we'll explore how AI can be used not only to streamline assessment tasks but also to fundamentally reimagine the feedback process in ways that promote deeper learning and student development.

The core aim of integrating AI in assessment and feedback is to create a more dynamic, responsive, and personalized learning environment. By harnessing AI's capabilities, educators can move beyond conventional, often time-intensive evaluation approaches to implement a more comprehensive and data-driven methodology. This transition enables real-time analysis of student work, instant feedback generation, and the ability to identify patterns and trends across entire groups, all while maintaining the crucial element of educator insight and judgment.

However, the path to incorporating AI into assessment practices comes with its own set of challenges and considerations. As we navigate this evolving field, it's crucial to find equilibrium between technological efficiency and the irreplaceable human element that defines effective teaching. This section will guide you through the process of thoughtfully integrating AI tools into your assessment strategy, ensuring that technology augments rather than replaces your professional expertise.

1. **Efficient Data Gathering with AI**
    - AI tools can be used to quickly assess student work, providing immediate feedback on various aspects such as accuracy, content understanding, and even creativity in some cases.
    - For example, in a language class, an AI tool could assess an essay for grammar, coherence, and style, whereas in a science class, it could evaluate the accuracy of answers and the logic used in problem solving.

2. **Personalizing Feedback**
    - The feedback provided by AI tools can be tailored to each student's performance. This might include highlighting specific areas of strength and suggesting focused improvements for areas of weakness.
    - Personalized comments generated by AI can address individual learning styles and needs, making the feedback more relevant and actionable for each student.
3. **Integrating Professional Judgment**
    - Even though AI provides quantitative data and initial feedback, your expertise as an educator is essential in interpreting this information in the context of each student's overall learning journey.
    - For instance, you might use AI-generated grades on a quiz as a starting point but supplement them with your observations of the student's engagement and understanding during classroom discussions or group work.
4. **Creating a Holistic Feedback Loop**
    - Combine the objective feedback from AI tools with subjective insights gained through classroom interactions. This approach offers students a comprehensive understanding of their performance.
    - Encourage students to reflect on both the AI-generated feedback and your observations. This can foster a deeper understanding of their learning process and areas for growth.
5. **Using AI Feedback to Guide Instruction**
    - Analyze the aggregated data from AI assessments to identify common areas where students struggle or excel. This can inform your teaching strategies and curriculum adjustments.
    - For example, if the AI tool consistently identifies a specific concept in math as a challenge for many students, you might decide to revisit that topic with additional instruction or resources.
6. **Regularly Updating Assessment Methods**
    - As AI tools evolve, continually explore new features or tools that could further enhance the assessment process.

- Stay informed about the latest advancements in educational AI and consider how they might be integrated into your assessment strategies to keep them effective and relevant.

By expanding your approach to assessment and feedback through the use of AI tools, you create a dynamic, responsive, and deeply informative educational experience. This approach not only streamlines the assessment process but also enriches it, ensuring that feedback is meaningful, timely, and conducive to student growth.

Reflective Practice

Reflective practice and continuous improvement are essential components in maximizing the benefits of AI-enhanced activities in the classroom. This approach goes beyond mere assessment; it represents a comprehensive method of constantly learning, adapting, and aligning AI tools with educational objectives. By engaging in reflective practice, you can fine-tune your teaching strategies and effectively respond to the ever-changing landscape of educational technology.

One of the most powerful ways to implement reflective practice is by conducting reflective sessions after each AI-enhanced activity. These sessions offer an opportunity for both educators and students to discuss what worked well and identify areas for improvement. Encouraging an open dialogue allows students to share their experiences honestly, providing valuable insights into how AI tools are affecting their learning. Questions such as "Which part of the AI activity captured your interest the most?" or "Were there any elements of the AI tool that you found challenging?" can help uncover critical feedback that may otherwise go unnoticed.

Gathering comprehensive student feedback is another crucial aspect of reflective practice. Offering multiple avenues for feedback, such as anonymous surveys, digital forms, and suggestion boxes, ensures that all students feel comfortable sharing their thoughts. This diverse collection of feedback allows you to gain a broader understanding of student perspectives. Although positive feedback can affirm the strengths of your teaching methods, negative feedback is equally important in highlighting areas that may need refinement or additional support.

The true value of feedback lies in transforming it into actionable insights. By analyzing common themes and patterns in student responses, you can identify specific aspects of AI tools that may need adjustments. For example, if students consistently struggle with a particular feature, it may indicate the need for clearer instructions or a more intuitive design. This process of analysis is essential for understanding the actual impact of AI on student learning and ensuring that the tools are being used to their full potential.

Armed with these insights, you can make evidence-based adjustments to your teaching methods and the AI tools themselves. This might involve experimenting with different formats or contexts for AI integration based on student feedback. For instance, if AI-driven quizzes are particularly well received, you might consider expanding their use across various subjects or incorporating them into group projects to foster collaboration.

Documenting the changes and observations that arise from reflective practice is another crucial step. Keeping detailed records not only helps track the effectiveness of AI integration over time but also provides a valuable resource for future reference. By regularly reviewing and updating these records, you can maintain a proactive approach to addressing new challenges and seizing opportunities in AI-enhanced education.

Professional development is also key to staying current with the latest advancements in AI and educational technology. Actively seeking out workshops, courses, and webinars can deepen your understanding of emerging tools and teaching methodologies. Engaging with a community of educators further enriches your practice by facilitating the exchange of innovative ideas and experiences.

By embedding reflective practice and continuous improvement into your approach, you ensure that AI integration in your classroom remains dynamic and adaptable. This method not only enhances your teaching effectiveness but also creates a learning environment that evolves alongside technological advancements. Ultimately, this approach helps you stay relevant, effective, and responsive to your students' diverse needs.

Scenario: Bridging Concepts and Technology with Ms. Patel

In this scenario, we delve into Ms. Patel's innovative approach to teaching geometry using an AI-based simulation. Her goal is to enhance her students' understanding of spatial relationships, a concept often challenging when taught through traditional methods. Ms. Patel starts by introducing an AI simulation tool to the class, such as GeoGebra or SketchUp, explaining its purpose and relevance to their current geometry topic. She demonstrates how the tool works, showcasing its features for manipulating and visualizing different geometric shapes and forms.

Recognizing her students' initial hesitation, Ms. Patel encourages them to start exploring the tool with a simple exercise: identifying and manipulating basic shapes. This guided exploration helps students become comfortable with the technology and its interface. As students become more engaged, Ms. Patel introduces more complex geometric concepts into the simulation. Students are tasked with visualizing and manipulating shapes to understand properties like volume, surface area, and the impact of transformations.

She uses real-world examples, asking students to model everyday objects using the simulation to illustrate how geometry is applied outside the classroom. Ms. Patel actively moves around the classroom, observing how students interact with the simulation. She pays attention to their problem-solving approaches and how they apply geometric concepts within the tool. She answers questions, provides hints, and encourages students to think critically about the geometric relationships they are exploring.

The AI tool's analytics feature allows Ms. Patel to track each student's progress. She identifies students who are excelling and those who might be struggling with specific concepts. For students who need additional support, she provides tailored instruction, either by spending more one-on-one time with them or by assigning supplementary exercises within the simulation.

Ms. Patel remains adaptable throughout the lesson, ready to address any technological issues that arise. For instance, if a student encounters a glitch with the simulation, she quickly troubleshoots the problem or provides an alternative approach. She seizes teachable moments, such as when a student makes a significant breakthrough in understanding, to reinforce concepts and inspire the rest of the class.

By the end of the lesson, Ms. Patel reviews the data collected by the AI tool and combines them with her observations to assess students' understanding of the spatial relationships. She reflects on the effectiveness of the lesson, considering how well the AI simulation facilitated learning and where improvements could be made for future lessons. Ms. Patel effectively bridges technology and geometry concepts, using the AI-based simulation as a dynamic tool to enhance learning. Her approach demonstrates how technology can transform abstract concepts into interactive and engaging learning experiences, yet her adaptability and use of AI analytics ensure that her teaching remains student-centered and effective.

Mastering the Balance, Facilitating the Future

As you conclude this chapter, you have likely successfully integrated AI into your classroom. This achievement signifies more than just adopting advanced technology; it marks a significant shift in your teaching approach, combining traditional methods with innovative AI tools. You have begun to master the balance between using technology and preserving the essence of conventional teaching. This balance enhances the learning experience, making it more interactive, personalized, and effective. The skills you've gained from implementing AI will help you make informed decisions about when and how to use technology to complement your teaching.

I also hope the insights from this chapter have empowered you to create a learning environment that is not only responsive to the needs of your students but also dynamic and engaging. The use of AI tools has opened up new avenues for interactive learning, allowing you to cater to various learning styles and paces. Your classroom has transformed into a space where technology supports and enhances learning outcomes, providing a rich and diverse experience.

The strategic use of AI tools in your teaching demonstrates a forward-thinking approach. You have learned to select and implement these tools in a way that complements your teaching objectives, rather than letting technology dictate the course of your curriculum. As you move forward, your newfound knowledge and experience with AI in education will guide you in fostering a classroom atmosphere that is both innovative and deeply rooted in effective teaching practices. Your classroom becomes a model of modern education, where students are not just consumers of information but active participants in a technologically enriched learning process.

The journey with AI in education is an ongoing one. Stay committed to learning and adapting, keeping abreast of the latest developments in educational technology and continually refining your approach to integrate these advancements effectively. Engage with a community of educators who are also exploring the use of AI in teaching to share experiences and insights.

In essence, integrating AI into your teaching is a step toward future-proofing education. It equips students with the skills and knowledge needed in a rapidly evolving digital world while maintaining the core values of traditional education. As you continue on this path, you become a facilitator of change, shaping a future where technology and education converge to create unlimited possibilities for student growth and learning.

6

Assessment and Reflection on AI-Enhanced Learning

ISTE EDUCATOR STANDARDS

2.1.a: Educators set professional learning goals to apply teaching practices made possible by technology, explore promising innovations, and reflect on their effectiveness.

2.7.c: Use assessment data to guide progress and communicate with students, parents, and education stakeholders to build student self-direction.

After discussing the implementation of AI-enhanced activities, this chapter focuses on the crucial stages of assessment and reflection. This chapter is dedicated to evaluating the effectiveness of AI integration in the classroom and reflecting on the learning outcomes. It emphasizes the importance of using assessment data to guide progress and communicate with stakeholders (Standard 2.7.c), ensuring that our students, their parents, and our colleagues understand the impact of AI tools on student growth.

Evaluating AI-enhanced activities and how well they have helped students learn is a crucial aspect of teaching with AI. This step is vital in understanding the effectiveness of AI integration in your teaching and its impact on student learning.

Evaluating AI-Enhanced Activities

Let's dive into the methodologies for collecting and analyzing data from AI-driven assessments, both formative and summative. I provide here guidance on how teachers can leverage these data to adapt their teaching methods, address individual student needs, and report progress to all invested parties:

1. **Planning Comprehensive Assessment of Learning Objectives**
   - Begin by revisiting the learning objectives you set out at the start of your AI-enhanced activities. Evaluation should be anchored in determining how well these objectives have been met.
   - Consider using a mixed-method approach for assessment. This means combining quantitative data from AI tools, such as quiz scores or analytics, with qualitative feedback from students and your own observations.
2. **Analyzing Student Performance Data**
   - Look closely at the performance data provided by AI tools. This could include scores from automated assessments, time spent on tasks, and patterns in student responses.
   - Analyze these data to identify trends and patterns. For example, are there specific concepts where students consistently perform well or struggle? Such insights can guide your future teaching strategies.
3. **Doing Qualitative Analysis of Engagement and Interaction**
   - Beyond the hard data, assess the qualitative aspects of student learning. This involves observing and reflecting on student engagement, participation, and interaction during AI-enhanced activities.
   - Conduct discussions or focus groups with students to gather their subjective experiences. Ask about their perceptions of the AI tools. Did they find them engaging, challenging, helpful, or frustrating?

4. **Assessing Impact on Understanding and Critical Thinking**
    - Evaluate whether the AI tools have contributed to a deeper understanding of the subject matter. Look for evidence of improved comprehension, application of concepts, and critical thinking in student work.
    - You might also assess the impact of AI tools on students' problem-solving skills and creativity. Have the tools encouraged students to think outside the box or approach problems in new ways?
5. **Examining Formative and Summative Assessment Data**
    - You should, of course, have used formative assessment throughout the learning process to gauge understanding and make real-time adjustments. This can include AI-generated quizzes, in-class activities, and informal feedback sessions.
    - Summative assessments, conducted at the end of a learning unit or term, should also be part of your evaluation. These can help you measure overall achievement and the long-term impact of AI-enhanced learning.
6. **Reflecting on Teacher's Role and Adjustments**
    - Reflect on your role in facilitating AI-enhanced activities. How effective were your strategies in integrating AI tools with traditional teaching methods?
    - Considering your reflections and evaluations, what adjustments might be needed in future iterations? This could involve changing the AI tools used, altering how they are integrated into lessons, or modifying your teaching approaches.

The evaluation of AI-enhanced activities is a multifaceted process that goes beyond mere data analysis. It requires a holistic approach that considers both quantitative and qualitative aspects of learning. By thoroughly assessing the impact of AI on student achievement and engagement, you can refine your teaching strategies, ensuring that AI tools are used in the most effective and pedagogically responsible manner. This chapter guides you through this crucial process, helping you harness the full potential of AI in your teaching journey.

Gathering and Incorporating Student Feedback

Effectively gathering and incorporating student feedback is crucial in evaluating and enhancing the use of AI tools in education. Here's a practical approach to collecting and analyzing student feedback, including a template for structuring this process.

1. **Develop a Feedback Mechanism**
   - Design Surveys: Create surveys tailored to gather specific insights about students' experiences with AI tools (like that shown in Figure 6.1). Surveys can include a mix of rating scales, multiple-choice questions, and open-ended questions for more detailed responses.
   - Digital Platforms for Feedback: Use digital platforms like Google Forms or SurveyMonkey for easy distribution and collection of feedback. This can streamline the process and encourage more students to participate.
   - Compile and Analyze Responses: Identify common themes and areas for improvement. Share key findings and potential changes with students to demonstrate that you are acting on their feedback. Continue to adapt and refine the use of AI tools in your classroom based on ongoing student feedback. By regularly implementing and reviewing such surveys, you can maintain a responsive and student-centered approach to the integration of AI tools in your instruction. Using this analysis, create an action plan that addresses the identified challenges and suggestions. This could involve adjusting how the AI tool is used in class, providing additional support or resources, or exploring alternative tools.
2. **Conduct Group Discussions**
   - Organize Classroom Discussions: Allocate time for classroom discussions where students can share their experiences using the AI tools. This can be in the form of a guided group discussion or more informal small-group chats.

FIGURE 6.1

Survey Template for AI Tool Feedback

Purpose:
This survey is designed to gather student feedback on the use of AI tools in the classroom. It aims to understand students' experiences, identify any challenges they encountered, and gather suggestions for improvement.

Instructions for Teachers:
Distribute this survey after students have had sufficient experience with the AI tool in your classroom. Encourage honest and thoughtful responses to get the most useful feedback. Assure students that their feedback is valuable and will be used to enhance their learning experience.

Survey:

Section 1—General Experience

Please rate your overall experience using the AI tool.

- ☐ Very Poor
- ☐ Poor
- ☐ Average
- ☐ Good
- ☐ Excellent

Section 2—Specific Features

Which features of the AI tool did you find most helpful? (Select all that apply)

- ☐ Real-time feedback
- ☐ Interactive simulations
- ☐ Personalized learning paths
- ☐ Automated grading
- ☐ Other (Please specify): ________

Section 3—Challenges Encountered

Describe any challenges you faced while using the AI tool. Please be as specific as possible.

Section 4—Learning Impact

How do you think the AI tool has affected your learning? Please provide specific examples if possible.

Section 5—Suggestions

Do you have any suggestions for how we can improve the use of this AI tool in our class? Your ideas and feedback are greatly appreciated.

   - Focus on Specific Aspects: Direct the discussion to focus on specific aspects of the AI tools, such as ease of use, areas of difficulty, perceived effectiveness in aiding learning, or suggestions for improvement.
3. **Facilitate Individual Reflections**
   - Reflection Prompts: Provide students with prompts for individual written reflections. These can be questions like "How did the AI tool affect your understanding of the topic?" or "What feature of the AI tool did you find most challenging or beneficial?"
   - Journaling: Encourage students to keep a journal of their experiences with the AI tools throughout the course. This can provide deeper insights into their learning journey.
4. **Follow Up on Feedback**
   - Communicate Changes: Inform students about the changes you plan to implement based on their feedback. This demonstrates that their input is valued and has a tangible impact on their learning environment.
   - Continuous Feedback Loop: Establish a continuous feedback loop, encouraging students to share their experiences as the implemented changes take effect. This ongoing dialogue ensures that the use of AI tools remains aligned with student needs and preferences.

By taking a structured and comprehensive approach to gathering and incorporating student feedback, you can gain valuable insights into the effectiveness of AI tools in your teaching. This process not only helps fine-tune the integration of technology into your classroom but also fosters a sense of collaboration and responsiveness, enhancing the overall learning experience.

Reflective Teaching Practice

Reflective teaching practice, especially in the realm of AI integration, is a process of continual learning and improvement. It involves critically examining your experiences with AI tools in the classroom and using these insights to refine your teaching strategies. Let's expand on how you can engage in reflective teaching practice, incorporating elements of the HAIL model for a comprehensive approach.

Facilitating Evaluation of AI Activities and Addressing Challenges

Here's how you can make the process of evaluating and refining your approach practical and effective, aligning with the HAIL model's principles. After each AI-enhanced lesson, review the clarity of your instructions. Were students able to follow them easily? Did they encounter any confusion? You might conduct brief follow-up surveys with students after using AI tools, asking them to rate their understanding of the tool and the clarity of your instructions. Include questions about both the technical and human aspects of the lesson, such as "How well did the AI tool help you understand the concept?" and "Did you feel supported by the teacher during the AI activity?"

Consider creating a checklist for future sessions that includes key points to cover when introducing the AI tool. This might involve step-by-step guidelines, common troubleshooting tips, and a Q&A session. Develop quick assessments or quizzes to gauge students' understanding of how to use the AI tools and identify areas where further instruction or clarification might be needed. These could be simple practical tasks or reflection questions that ask students to explain how they would use specific features of the tool.

Reflect on how well you balanced the human aspects of teaching with the integration of AI tools. Did you maintain regular personal interactions and discussions, or did the technology dominate the classroom environment? In future sessions, aim to consciously alternate between direct instruction and AI tool usage, ensuring that students receive a balanced learning experience.

Keep a detailed log of any challenges that arise during AI-enhanced activities. Categorize these challenges into technical issues, student engagement concerns, or instructional difficulties. After each lesson, review this log and analyze the challenges that arose. Were they isolated incidents, or do they indicate a pattern that needs addressing?

Reflect on Your Problem-Solving Strategies

For each noted challenge, document the solutions you tried. Did you employ innovative approaches, perhaps using different features of the AI tool, or did you revert to more traditional methods to address the issue? Reflect on the effectiveness of these solutions. For example, if a technical glitch disrupted a lesson, did your backup plan maintain the continuity of learning?

When reflecting on your problem-solving strategies, consider how they align with the Augment and Leverage stages of the HAIL model. Did you use AI to enhance the learning experience while also leveraging your expertise and experience as an educator to navigate challenges? Moving forward, plan strategies that use both the strengths of AI tools and your own teaching skills. For instance, if an AI tool isn't effectively engaging students, consider complementing it with hands-on activities or group discussions that you facilitate.

You might also organize regular reflection sessions with fellow educators, sharing experiences and strategies for integrating AI into the classroom. Use these sessions to brainstorm solutions to common challenges and to share tips for maintaining a balance between AI tools and traditional teaching methods.

By taking a structured, reflective approach to evaluating your facilitation of AI activities and addressing challenges, you can continuously improve your teaching methods. This process ensures that AI tools are integrated effectively into your teaching, enhancing the learning experience while staying true to the core principles of the HAIL model.

Try Using a Template for Self-Review

After each AI-enhanced lesson, take time for a thorough self-review. Reflect on the effectiveness of the AI tool used and the methods of implementation. Were the learning objectives met? How did students respond to the AI integration? You might consider creating a structured template for this review, such as those shown in Figures 6.2 and 6.3, focusing on key areas like student engagement, ease of use of the tool, and the achievement of learning outcomes.

FIGURE 6.2

Self-Review of AI-Enhanced Lesson

This template is designed to facilitate a structured self-review and reflection after conducting AI-enhanced lessons. It aims to assess the effectiveness of the AI tool used, evaluate the methods of implementation, and gather insights for future improvements.

Lesson Details:

Date:

AI Tool Used:

Lesson Topic:

AI Tool Effectiveness:

- Did the AI tool function as expected during the lesson?
- Were there any technical issues? If so, how were they resolved?

Implementation Methods:

- How was the AI tool introduced and integrated into the lesson?
- Were the instructions clear and easy to follow for the students?

Learning Objectives:

- List the learning objectives for the lesson.
- Were these objectives met? Provide specific examples.

Student Engagement and Response:

- How did the students respond to the AI integration?
- Were the students actively engaged? Note any observations.

Challenges Encountered:

- What challenges did you face during the lesson (technical, engagement, instructional)?
- How did you address these challenges?

Reflections and Future Improvements:

- What aspects of the AI integration worked well?
- What would you do differently in future implementations?

FIGURE 6.3

Collecting and Reflecting on Student Feedback

Feedback Collection Method:
How was student feedback collected? (e.g., survey, group discussion)

Date of Feedback Collection:

Summary of Student Feedback:
- Key points from the feedback regarding the AI tool and its impact on learning.
- Any specific suggestions or concerns raised by the students.

Reflections on Student Feedback:
- How does the feedback align with your observations?
- What insights can be drawn from the feedback for future lessons?

Actionable Steps:
- Considering the self-review and student feedback, list actionable steps for improvement.
- Include any changes to AI tool selection, teaching methods, or lesson plans.

Additional Notes:
Any other observations or thoughts related to the lesson and AI integration.

It's important to regularly review this template after AI-enhanced lessons and use the insights gained to adjust your teaching approach and AI tool usage. This template serves as a comprehensive tool to guide reflective practice and gather actionable feedback, ensuring that AI integration in your classroom is continually assessed, refined, and optimized for the best educational outcomes. Continually refine this template, or how you use it, to align with your classroom's evolving needs.

Adjusting AI Tool Selection and Usage

Considering your reflections, determine whether a different AI tool might be more effective or if the current tool could be used differently. For instance, if an AI-based quiz tool isn't engaging enough, consider an AI tool that offers interactive simulations. Experiment with various AI tools and observe which ones resonate best with your students and align with your teaching style. Reflect on how to better balance AI with traditional teaching. This might involve integrating AI tools as a complement to classroom discussions or group activities, rather than as standalone elements.

Use the HAIL model as a guide to navigate this balance. For example, if you've been heavily leveraging AI, consider incorporating more humanizing elements in your next lesson, such as group discussions or personal storytelling. Be sure to employ more humanizing methods to collect student feedback also, such as using informal group discussions or individual interviews as well as digital surveys. This diversity in feedback collection can provide a more comprehensive view of student experiences. Keep the HAIL model in mind as you analyze student feedback. For instance, if students report feeling overwhelmed by the technology, this indicates a need to emphasize the Humanize aspect more.

Student feedback can help you gauge where on the HAIL continuum your current approach lies and adjust accordingly. If students crave more interactive experiences, for instance, look into AI tools that offer a higher degree of student interaction (Augment and Integrate aspects). Keep a dedicated journal or digital log for reflections on AI integration. After each AI-enhanced lesson, record your observations, student feedback, and your thoughts on the effectiveness of the AI tools.

This journal should document not only what happened but also your responses to various situations, the decisions you made, and the rationale behind those decisions. Regularly review your journal entries to identify patterns or recurring themes. This can help you recognize areas of strength in your AI integration strategy and pinpoint aspects that need improvement. For example, if you notice a pattern where student engagement drops during certain AI-based activities, consider exploring new ways to use AI that better capture student interest.

By expanding your practice to include these reflective and feedback-focused strategies, you lay the groundwork for continual improvement in AI integration, ensuring that your teaching remains dynamic, responsive, and aligned with the evolving needs of your students and the new possibilities for AI in education.

Professional Development and Continuous Learning

To remain effective and relevant in the evolving landscape of educational technology, continuous professional development is crucial. Here's how you can actively engage in professional development opportunities and use them to enhance your AI integration strategies, aligning with the HAIL model's principles:

1. **Identify Relevant Professional Development Opportunities**
   - Seek out workshops, webinars, and conferences specifically focused on AI in education. These can provide you with the latest insights, tools, and strategies for integrating AI into your teaching.
   - Consider joining professional learning communities or online forums where educators discuss and share experiences about using AI in the classroom. This can be a rich source of practical tips and innovative ideas.
2. **Participate in Collaborative Projects**
   - Do collaborative projects with other educators to experiment with and implement AI tools in diverse settings. This collaboration can offer a broader perspective and help you understand different ways to use AI effectively.
   - Look for opportunities to collaborate with tech companies or universities at the forefront of AI in education. This can provide access to cutting-edge tools and resources.

3. **Apply Learning to Practice**
    - After attending a professional development session, plan how you will apply what you've learned to your teaching. This might involve experimenting with a new AI tool, adapting a new teaching strategy, or even redesigning a lesson plan to better integrate AI.
    - Reflect on how these new approaches align with the HAIL model. Are they helping to humanize the learning experience, augment your teaching, integrate seamlessly, and leverage AI's full potential?
4. **Share Knowledge and Experiences**
    - Share your learning and experiences with your colleagues by having informal discussions, leading a professional development session, or contributing to a shared resource repository.
    - By sharing, you not only reinforce your own learning but also contribute to creating a community of practice that values continual growth and adaptation in the field of educational technology.
5. **Document and Track Your Professional Growth**
    - Keep a record of your professional development activities and reflections through a portfolio, blog, or journal.
    - Regularly review this documentation to assess your growth over time and identify areas for future development.

By actively engaging in professional development and continuous learning, you not only enhance your skills and knowledge in AI integration but also contribute to a learning environment that is dynamic, responsive, and attuned to the students' needs. This commitment to growth ensures that your teaching practices remain at the cutting edge of educational technology and pedagogy.

Continuous Improvement in AI-Enhanced Teaching

The journey of integrating AI into your teaching is an ongoing process that requires a commitment to continuous improvement. This involves not only adapting your current practices but also seeking new opportunities for growth and learning. It's best to develop a structured plan for continuous improvement in your AI-enhanced teaching approach.

Start by reviewing the assessments and reflections from your AI-enhanced lessons. Identify key areas for improvement, such as student engagement levels, the effectiveness of the AI tools used, or your own proficiency in using these tools. Set specific, measurable goals for improvement. For instance, if student engagement is low, a goal could be to find and integrate an AI tool that better aligns with student interests or learning styles.

Consider undergoing additional training or professional development to enhance your understanding and skills in using AI in education, using the suggestions mentioned in the previous section. Actively seek out resources and learning materials that can deepen your knowledge about the latest AI tools and their applications to stay up-to-date on the rapidly evolving field of educational technology.

As you ponder the role of AI in your instructional toolkit, it is vital to stay informed about the perceived impact of the latest developments on the learning landscape. García-Peñalvo (2023) discusses the complex perceptions of artificial intelligence in education, especially after the advent of groundbreaking tools like ChatGPT, highlighting a spectrum of reactions from disruption to panic. Those insights might prompt a deeper reflection on how your instructional methods can adapt to integrate AI effectively. You might begin by experimenting with many diverse AI tools, initiating pilot tests to evaluate their pedagogical value before a full-scale implementation, and adjusting your teaching strategies to incorporate more use of AI. To support students navigating AI, develop comprehensive guides and establish support systems, such as peer mentoring, while also seeking professional development opportunities to enhance your own understanding.

By adopting a mindset of continuous improvement, you not only enhance your teaching practice but also ensure that your approach to integrating AI remains innovative, effective, and responsive to your students' needs. This proactive stance helps you make the most of the opportunities AI presents to enrich the learning experience.

Adapting AI Strategies Based on Reflection

The process of adapting your AI strategies based on reflections and student feedback is a dynamic and continuous practice. To make this process practical and effective, follow the steps shown in Figures 6.4 and 6.5.

FIGURE 6.4

Reflections to Action

Date of Review:

Summary of Reflections:
Key observations from personal reflections on AI-enhanced lessons.

Summary of Student Feedback:
Key points from student feedback regarding the AI tool's use and effectiveness.

Areas Identified for Adaptation:
Specific aspects of AI use needing change (e.g., tool navigation, engagement level).

Developing a Change Plan

Objectives for Change:
Clear goals for what the changes aim to achieve.

Steps for Implementation:

Step-by-Step Action Plan

Action:
Timeline:
Resources needed:
Pilot Testing (if applicable):

Plan for conducting a pilot test of the changes:
Group/Class for Pilot:
Duration:
Specific focus of the test:

FIGURE 6.5

Implementing the Changes

Implementation of Changes

Date of Implementation:

Observations during implementation:

Review and Feedback Post-Implementation:

Date of Review:

Feedback from students post-implementation:

Teacher's observations and reflections:

Adjustments Post-Review:

Necessary adjustments identified from the review:

Adjustment:

Planned Implementation Date:

Ongoing Review and Update

Scheduled Review Dates:

Dates set for future reviews of AI strategy effectiveness:

Criteria for Future Reviews:

Specific criteria to evaluate the effectiveness of the adapted AI strategies:

Documentation and Sharing

Record of Adaptations and Outcomes:

Document the changes made, challenges encountered, solutions implemented, and observed outcomes:

Sharing with Professional Community:

Plan for sharing experiences and learnings with colleagues:

Platform/Method of Sharing:

Date/Period:

Complete each section of the template after an AI-enhanced lesson or series of lessons and use the information gathered to inform and guide the adaptation of AI strategies in your teaching. It's important to regularly update and review this document to track progress and make continuous improvements.

Refining the Digital Classroom with Mr. Jenkins

In this scenario, we explore how Mr. Jenkins, a high school teacher, navigates the challenges of integrating AI into his language arts classroom. Initially, he implemented a system that incorporated several AI-based tools with the hope of enhancing his students' learning experience. A few weeks into the program, Mr. Jenkins decides to evaluate its effectiveness. He conducts an assessment of his students' work, focusing on both the technical aspects of grammar and the more subjective elements of creative writing. Using an AI tool, he gathers quantitative data on their grammatical proficiency and takes the time to manually review their creative pieces for a qualitative understanding of their progress. He discovers that integrating AI has significantly improved students' grammar skills, but it hasn't made a similar impact on their creative writing abilities. This revelation prompts him to engage in a reflective process, aiming to understand the root of this issue.

Seeking deeper insights, Mr. Jenkins turns to his students for feedback. He organizes sessions during which they openly discuss their experiences with the AI system. He learns that even though the students appreciate the structured guidance on grammar, they feel constrained in their creative expression due to the AI tool's rigid approach.

Armed with this feedback, Mr. Jenkins adjusts his teaching strategy. He revises his lesson plans to include more open-ended writing activities, encouraging students to explore various themes and express their creativity freely. He designs prompts that stimulate imagination, allowing students to delve into storytelling and narrative exploration without the confines of strict AI guidelines.

Despite these changes, Mr. Jenkins continues to use the AI tool for feedback purposes. He tweaks its settings to focus more on encouraging stylistic diversity and creativity rather than just adhering to grammatical accuracy. In class, he allocates time for students to discuss the AI feedback, aiming to deepen their understanding of how it can enhance their creative writing.

In his revised approach, Mr. Jenkins strikes a balance between the structured practice offered by AI and the creative freedom of traditional writing exercises. This balance aligns with the principles of the HAIL model, particularly in integrating technology in a way that humanizes the learning experience. He plans to closely monitor the impact of these changes, observing both student engagement and the quality of their creative writing.

Mr. Jenkins is committed to an ongoing process of evaluation and adaptation. He understands that effective teaching strategies require continual refinement, and he remains open to further adjustments based on student performance and feedback. His approach exemplifies the adaptive, reflective methodology essential for the successful integration of AI in education.

A Continuous Cycle of Reflection and Improvement

In this chapter, you explored the critical process of assessment and reflection, which is essential for effectively integrating AI into your teaching. This process highlights the importance of an ongoing cycle: assessing learning outcomes, gathering and interpreting feedback, reflecting on your teaching methods, and making necessary adjustments. Through this continuous cycle, AI moves beyond being just a tool and becomes a key part of the education experience. This is not a one-time task but an ongoing practice, crucial for staying up-to-date with the fast-paced developments in AI and its role in education.

The insights you've gathered throughout this chapter should serve as a robust foundation for fostering a learning environment that's both reflective and adaptable. As you delve deeper into the use of AI in your teaching, it's crucial to maintain this cycle of reflection and adaptation. By doing so, you ensure that the AI tools and strategies you employ are always aligned with your students' evolving needs and your curriculum objectives. Remember, the goal of integrating AI in education is not just about harnessing its technological prowess but about enhancing the overall learning experience in a manner that is responsive, student-centric, and pedagogically sound.

As you continue to navigate the changing landscape of AI in teaching, this chapter will serve as a key reference point. It offers a framework for ensuring the AI tools you thoughtfully integrate into your teaching repertoire contribute positively to your students' learning journeys. The principles and practices discussed here will guide you in making informed decisions about using AI, helping you strike the right balance between technology and traditional teaching methods. Embrace this journey as an opportunity for professional growth and innovation, with the aim of enriching the tapestry for all students.

7

Fostering a Culture of Continuous Improvement in AI Integration

ISTE EDUCATOR STANDARDS

2.1.b: Pursue professional interests by creating and actively participating in local and global learning networks.

2.2.a: Shape, advance, and accelerate a shared vision for empowered learning with technology by engaging with education stakeholders.

In this final chapter, we turn our attention to the philosophy of continuous improvement in the use of AI in education. Here, we explore how to sustain momentum, update lesson plans based on feedback, and stay current with evolving AI tools and pedagogical strategies. To do so, it's good to participate in local and global learning networks (Standard 2.1.b) to share insights, learn from the collective experience, and continuously refine your approach to AI integration.

This chapter is about nurturing a culture in which innovation is ongoing and AI's educational value is perpetually enhanced. It's also about fostering socially responsible contributions in the digital world (Standard 2.2.a), guiding students to become thoughtful citizens in a technologically advanced society.

Incorporating AI effectively into your teaching demands a mindset of growth and adaptability. This mindset isn't limited to your students—it starts with you, the educator. Embracing change as an integral part of the learning journey is crucial. Each challenge encountered should be viewed not as a setback but as a valuable opportunity for learning and improvement.

Reflecting on Change and Setting Goals in AI-Enhanced Education

Pause to Reflect

When faced with the introduction of a new AI tool or an unexpected outcome from trying a teaching method, pause and reflect. Consider each new challenge or change as an opportunity for growth rather than a setback. This mindset is essential to the Humanize aspect of the HAIL model, where empathy and understanding toward oneself and students play a crucial role. By reflecting on your experiences, you engage in a process that values the human element in teaching, acknowledging that growth often comes from overcoming obstacles.

Ask yourself reflective questions such as "What insights can I gain from this situation?" or "How can this experience enhance my teaching practice?" Asking such questions encourages a deeper engagement with the Augment and Integrate aspects of the HAIL model, allowing you to enhance your capabilities with AI while ensuring that it complements rather than replaces the human touch in education.

After reflecting, continue to leverage AI to support and extend initiatives, pushing the boundaries of what's possible in the classroom and beyond. Involve students in the reflective process, encouraging them to consider the implications of AI in their learning and the broader digital landscape. This not only prepares them for the future but also instills a sense of responsibility as they interact with technology. Through continuous reflection and engagement with learning networks, your pedagogical practice becomes a living, evolving entity, responsive to your students' needs and the demands of a constantly changing world.

Set Personal Goals for Continuous Learning

Developing personal goals for continuous learning and development is pivotal to effectively integrate AI into your curriculum. Some of these goals should align with the Leverage stage of the HAIL model, where you can use AI's full potential to craft personalized and engaging learning experiences.

1. **Short-Term Goals**
   - Identify specific AI tools or features you aim to master in the upcoming semester. Such goals could range from understanding the basics of an AI-driven content delivery platform to employing AI-based analytics for assessing student progress.
   - Plan to attend a certain number of webinars or workshops focused on AI in education, aiming to broaden your understanding and stay up-to-date with the latest developments.
2. **Long-Term Goals**
   - Consider more ambitious objectives, such as integrating a comprehensive AI-driven project into your curriculum or collaborating with colleagues on interdisciplinary AI-based teaching initiatives.
   - Aim to contribute to the field by sharing your experiences and insights through professional networks, publications, or conferences, thereby enriching the broader education community.

As you set personal goals, ensure that they are in harmony with the HAIL model (see Figure 7.1). For instance, if your aim is to master a new AI tool each semester, consider how this tool will contribute to humanizing the learning process or augmenting your teaching capabilities. If you intend to delve into AI's ethical implications, reflect on how this understanding will integrate into your curriculum to provide a holistic learning experience that goes beyond the syllabus. It's good to document these goals in a professional development plan, aligning each with a stage of the HAIL model.

By engaging in this reflective practice and setting clear, actionable goals, you ensure that your journey with AI in education is not only about adopting new technologies but also about fostering personal and professional growth—and that your AI integration will be a thoughtful, enriching, and human-centered endeavor.

FIGURE 7.1

Personal Goals Template for AI-Enhanced Education

Name:

Date:

Short-Term Goals

AI Tool Mastery

Tool/Feature:

Action Plan:

Deadline:

Professional Development

Event/Resource:

Action Plan:

Deadline:

Long-Term Goals

Curriculum Integration

Project/Initiative:

Action Plan:

Deadline:

(*continued*)

FIGURE 7.1 (*continued*)

Personal Goals Template for AI-Enhanced Education

Community Contribution

Platform/Format:

Action Plan:

Deadline:

Reflection:

Challenges Encountered

Description:

Learning Outcomes:

Successes Achieved:

Description:

Creating a Collaborative Learning Culture

Encourage a culture of sharing and collaboration among your colleagues. Organize regular meetings or workshops where you can share experiences, challenges, and successes in integrating AI into the classroom. You might use these gatherings to discuss how the HAIL model can be practically applied in different teaching scenarios; for instance, how can AI be used to augment a traditional lesson plan, or what are the best practices for integrating AI tools while maintaining a strong human connection with students?

It's good to regularly review your lesson plans and teaching strategies through the lens of the HAIL model. Ask yourself, "Am I effectively balancing humanizing and leveraging aspects of AI in my teaching?" This reflective practice ensures that your approach remains dynamic and responsive.

You can cultivate a growth mindset in your students by modeling this behavior. Share your learning experiences with AI, including challenges and how you overcame them. Design classroom activities that encourage students to experiment with AI tools, promoting a trial-and-error approach. Frame challenges as learning opportunities, fostering an environment where students feel safe to take risks and explore.

Using Professional Development Resources

In the rapidly advancing field of AI in education, continuous professional development is essential for staying informed and effectively integrating these technologies into your teaching practice. By systematically pursuing professional development in AI and sharing your newfound knowledge with your colleagues and students, you contribute to a culture of continuous learning and innovation. A commitment to ongoing learning not only enhances your teaching but also ensures that AI is integrated in a manner that aligns with the HAIL model—a model that respects the human essence at the core of education while harnessing the capabilities of technology. Here are some kinds of professional development you can actively pursue and leverage to enhance your—and your education community's—understanding of AI.

1. **Online Courses**
    - Look for reputable online platforms offering courses in AI applications in education. These courses can range from introductory to advanced levels, catering to your specific needs and expertise level.
    - Prioritize courses that offer practical insights and hands-on experience with AI tools relevant to your teaching discipline.
2. **Conferences and Seminars**
    - Identify key educational technology conferences that have a focus on AI. Many conferences offer both in-person and virtual attendance options.

- Plan to attend sessions or workshops specifically dedicated to AI in education, noting those that offer case studies, research findings, or practical teaching strategies.

3. **Webinars and Workshops**
   - Join or subscribe to educational technology organizations or AI tool providers that regularly host webinars and workshops.
   - Allocate time in your schedule to attend these sessions, focusing on those that promise actionable insights and direct applications to your teaching context.
4. **Knowledge-Sharing Sessions**
   - Organize regular knowledge-sharing sessions with your colleagues where you can discuss key takeaways from your professional development activities.
   - Use these sessions to brainstorm how new AI insights and tools can be integrated into your school or department's curriculum.
5. **Sharing with Students**
   - Share relevant AI concepts and tools with your students, perhaps through dedicated seminars or as part of existing courses.
   - Encourage students to explore these AI tools and consider their implications for the subject matter being taught.

To identify professional development opportunities that will be relevant to you, start by identifying opportunities that allow you to explore the Humanize aspect of AI—those that help you understand how AI can support the emotional and social dimensions of learning. Seek workshops that discuss the ethical use of AI and its potential to foster empathy and understanding in students. This will enable you to maintain the human touch in an increasingly digital classroom.

For PD that supports the Augment phase, focus on training sessions that enhance your abilities to integrate AI in a way that supports and strengthens your teaching methods. These could include courses on adaptive learning technologies that tailor educational experiences to individual student needs without losing the personal connection that characterizes impactful teaching.

To support the Integrate aspect, look for PD that teaches seamless incorporation of AI into existing pedagogical practices. Prioritize learning that helps technology become an extension of your teaching, enriching the learning experience in a natural and intuitive way, such as workshops on blended learning environments or AI tools that complement traditional instruction.

PD that supports the Leverage stage will encourage you to explore the cutting edge of AI-driven education. Engage in advanced courses that explore predictive analytics, AI-driven personalization, and the creation of intelligent learning pathways. This knowledge will allow you to anticipate trajectories and tailor learning experiences, ensuring that students are active participants in their education journey. By approaching professional development through the lens of the HAIL model, you ensure that your growth as an educator not only keeps pace with technological advances but also retains the core values of empathy, connection, and personal engagement. This balanced approach positions you at the vanguard of innovation in education.

It's important to document and keep a record of your professional development activities (see Figure 7.2). This can include certificates of completion, notes from sessions attended, and reflections on your learning. Review and update your professional development plan regularly to ensure that it remains aligned with your evolving teaching needs and the advancements in AI technology.

Updating and Refining AI-Enhanced Lesson Plans

As you accumulate more experience using AI in teaching, it's essential to periodically revisit and refine your lesson plans. This practice ensures that your AI use remains aligned with goals and adapts to your students' changing needs. Here are practical steps for updating and refining your AI-enhanced lesson plans.

1. **Conduct Regular Lesson Plan Reviews**
    - Schedule periodic reviews of your lesson plans, perhaps at the end of each unit or semester. During these reviews, assess the effectiveness of the AI tools and activities you've integrated.
    - Look at student performance data, feedback, and your own observations to identify areas where the AI tools were most and least effective.

FIGURE 7.2

Professional Development Tracker Template

Name:

Academic Year:

Professional Development Plan:

Activity Type	Title/Topic	Provider	Date	Objectives	Application/ Strategy	Reflections
Online Course	Example: "AI in Education: The Basics and Beyond"	Example: Coursera	Start: End:	To gain a foundational understanding of AI applications in education.	Integrate an AI-based quiz tool into history lessons to enhance student engagement.	Reflections on course content, ease of tool integration, student response, and areas for further exploration.
Conference	Example: "EdTech Innovators Summit 2025"	EdTech Global	Date:	To explore the latest AI tools and network with other educators.	Share insights with the department and pilot a new AI discussion platform in the classroom.	Insights gained from networking, effectiveness of the new tool, and student feedback.
Webinar	Example: "Maximizing AI for Personalized Learning"	AIEdTech Co.	Date:	To understand how AI can personalize learning experiences.	Implement personalized learning paths in the next unit using an AI learning platform.	Student engagement levels, personalization success, and areas for improvement.

Notes:

* This tracker should be updated regularly as you plan, attend, and reflect on professional development activities.
* After each activity, take time to jot down key insights, potential applications in your teaching practice, and any follow-up actions you plan to take.

2. **Incorporate Feedback and Data into Revisions**
   - Analyze student feedback regarding their experiences with the AI tools. Pay attention to their insights on what worked well and what didn't.
   - Use any quantitative data provided by the AI tools, such as student engagement metrics or performance analytics, to understand how these tools are affecting learning.
3. **Adjust AI Integration Based on Findings**
   - If certain AI activities were highly effective, consider how they can be expanded or replicated in other areas of your teaching. For instance, if an AI tool that facilitates personalized learning in math was successful, explore how a similar approach could be applied in other subjects.
   - Conversely, if some AI tools didn't yield the desired outcomes, contemplate reducing their usage or replacing them with alternative methods or tools. Sometimes, traditional teaching methods are more effective in achieving certain learning objectives.
4. **Experiment with Different AI Tools and Approaches**
   - Stay open to experimenting with new AI tools that might better suit your goals. The field of AI in education is rapidly evolving, and new tools are constantly emerging.
   - Try out different ways of integrating AI into your lessons. For example, use AI tools for group activities to foster collaborative learning or for individual assignments to support personalized learning paths.
5. **Enhance AI Activities with Additional Support**
   - If students struggle with certain AI-enhanced tasks, consider providing additional scaffolding or support.
   - Regularly check in with your students to gauge their comfort and proficiency with the AI tools, adjusting your support accordingly.
6. **Document Changes and Monitor Outcomes**
   - Keep a record of the changes you make to your lesson plans and the reasons behind these changes. This documentation can be valuable for future reference and for sharing best practices with colleagues.

- Monitor the outcomes of these changes over time to assess their impact. This ongoing evaluation will help you make informed decisions about future AI integration in your lesson plans.

Exploring New AI Tools and Resources

Staying current with the latest advancements in AI tools and resources is crucial for keeping your teaching methods fresh and effective. Try these practical steps and tools to navigate the evolving landscape of AI in education.

1. **Scheduled Exploration Time**
   - Set aside regular time in your schedule specifically for exploring new AI tools and resources. This could be a few hours every week or a dedicated day each month.
   - Use this time to research the latest AI developments, read educational technology blogs, or explore new tools that have entered the market. You might subscribe to educational technology journals, newsletters, or online publications that regularly cover AI advancements and case studies in education. Read and reflect on these publications during your scheduled exploration time.
2. **Engagement with Professional Learning Networks**
   - Join online forums, social media groups, or professional networks that focus on AI in education. Platforms like LinkedIn, X (formerly known as Twitter), and specialized educational technology forums can be valuable sources of information and community support. Attending conferences and webinars is also a good way to learn about new tools.
   - Engage actively in these networks by asking questions, sharing your experiences, and discussing the latest AI tools and strategies with peers.
3. **Tool Exploration Template**
   - Create an AI tool exploration template (see Figure 7.3) to systematically evaluate new AI tools. This template should include criteria such as ease of use, cost, compatibility with existing technology, and relevance to your curriculum.
   - Use this template every time you explore a new tool to ensure a consistent and thorough evaluation.

4. **Pilot Testing of New Tools**
   - Select promising AI tools for pilot testing in your classroom. Start with small-scale implementations to gauge the tool's effectiveness and student response.
   - Collect feedback from students and observe how the tool affects learning outcomes. Use these data to decide whether to adopt the tool more broadly.

FIGURE 7.3

AI Tool Exploration Template

This template is designed to facilitate a systematic evaluation of new AI tools for educational purposes. Use this template to assess each tool's fit and potential impact on your teaching and learning environment.

Tool Name:
Provider/Developer:
Tool URL:
Date of Evaluation:
Evaluator:

Evaluation Criteria

1. Ease of Use:
   - User Interface:
   - Learning Curve:
   - Documentation/Support:
2. Cost:
   - Free or Paid:
   - Subscription Model:
   - Institutional Licensing Options:
3. Compatibility:
   - With Existing Technology:
   - Integration Capabilities:

(continued)

FIGURE 7.3 (*continued*)

AI Tool Exploration Template

4. Relevance to Curriculum:
   - Applicability to Subject Matter:
   - Enhancement of Learning Objectives:
5. Pedagogical Value:
   - Supports Differentiated Learning:
   - Engages Students:
   - Promotes Collaboration:
6. Data Privacy and Security:
   - Compliance with Standards:
   - Data Handling Policies:

Overall Assessment

- Strengths:
- Weaknesses:
- Potential Use Cases in Curriculum:

Decision

- Adopt:
- Further Exploration Needed:
- Not Suitable at This Time:

Additional Notes:

Sharing and Reflecting:

Share your findings and experiences with new AI tools during staff meetings or professional development sessions. This not only helps others but also reinforces your own learning. Reflect on how each new tool aligns with the HAIL model.

Scenario: Continuous Improvement in Action

Dr. Ellis, a seasoned history teacher, embarked on a journey to integrate AI into her classroom to enhance her students' engagement with historical texts. She introduced an AI-powered tool designed to aid in the analysis of these texts, hoping to deepen her students' understanding of historical contexts and perspectives.

As the semester unfolded, Dr. Ellis took proactive steps to assess the effectiveness of this new technology in her teaching arsenal. Midway through the semester, she conducted a thorough evaluation of the AI tool's impact. She analyzed students' performance data, looking for improvements in their analytical skills and overall comprehension of historical materials. To gain more nuanced insights, Dr. Ellis also sought direct feedback from her students. She organized a feedback session, inviting open and honest discussions about their experiences with the AI tool.

The feedback was revealing. Even though students found the tool helpful in breaking down complex texts, many expressed difficulties in navigating its features, suggesting a need for a more user-friendly interface. Determined to optimize the use of AI in her classroom, Dr. Ellis decided to further her own education. She enrolled in a professional development workshop focused on digital literacy and AI applications in education. The workshop proved to be an eye-opener, providing her with fresh insights into effectively integrating technology into teaching. She learned new strategies for scaffolding the use of AI tools, ensuring that students not only used the tool but also fully understood its workings and potential benefits.

The workshop also introduced Dr. Ellis to a range of alternative AI resources. She explored these new tools, assessing their suitability for her classroom needs. She looked for tools that promised a more intuitive user interface, in consideration of the feedback from her students. After careful consideration, Dr. Ellis decided to pilot one of these new tools, intending to compare its effectiveness against the original tool she had used.

Back in her classroom, Dr. Ellis implemented the new strategies she had learned. She redesigned her lesson plans to include more structured guidance on using the AI tool. This involved creating step-by-step tutorials and interactive demos and setting aside time in her lessons for students to experiment with the tool under her supervision. Dr. Ellis also introduced the new AI tool she had discovered, keen to see if its user-friendly design would resonate better with her students.

As the semester drew to a close, Dr. Ellis reflected on the path she had charted. The journey was a blend of challenges and achievements, but it underscored the importance of adaptability and continuous learning in the effective use of AI in education. Dr. Ellis's story serves as a testament to the evolving nature of teaching, highlighting the need for educators to remain students themselves—always learning, adapting, and evolving to meet the needs of their students in an ever-changing landscape.

Implementing Feedback Loops

Establishing effective feedback loops is a crucial component for the continuous improvement of AI-integrated lessons. These loops should encompass a wide range of perspectives, including students, colleagues, and your own self-reflection. Here's how to create and implement these feedback loops in a practical and systematic manner.

1. **Student Feedback Collection**
    - Develop regular mechanisms for collecting student feedback on AI-enhanced lessons. This could include digital surveys, suggestion boxes, or dedicated time in class for open discussions.
    - Tailor your feedback tools to be age-appropriate and ensure that they can capture both quantitative data (like ratings) and qualitative insights (like open-ended responses).

   - Encourage honest and constructive feedback by creating an environment where students feel their opinions are valued and will be acted on.
2. **Peer Review System**
   - Establish a peer review system through which fellow educators observe your AI-integrated lessons and provide feedback. This can be a reciprocal arrangement, offering a valuable opportunity for mutual learning and growth.
   - Create a structured observation guide that focuses on specific aspects of AI integration, such as how effectively the AI tool is being used, student engagement levels, and the overall integration of the tool into the lesson plan.
3. **Self-Evaluation**
   - After each AI-enhanced lesson, take time for self-reflection. Consider maintaining a teaching journal where you can jot down your observations, thoughts, and ideas for improvement.
   - Reflect on aspects such as your comfort level with the AI tool, its impact on lesson dynamics, and areas where you feel the integration could be improved.
4. **Reviewing the Feedback**
   - Consolidate the feedback from all sources and review it regularly. Look for common themes, areas for improvement, and successful practices that can be replicated or expanded.
   - Use this consolidated feedback to inform your lesson planning. Make necessary adjustments to the AI tools or your teaching strategies based on this feedback.
5. **Action Plan and Implementation**
   - Develop an action plan based on the feedback. This plan should include specific changes or improvements you will make, along with timelines and responsible parties (if applicable). Implement the changes in your subsequent lessons and monitor the outcomes.
   - Be prepared to make further adjustments based on the ongoing feedback and observations.

6. **Communicate the Changes**
    - Communicate any changes you make in your lessons to your students and colleagues. Let them know that their feedback has been heard and is valued.
    - This communication not only fosters a sense of community and collaboration but also enhances the effectiveness of the feedback loop by encouraging continued participation.

By implementing such structured feedback loops, you ensure that your AI-integrated lessons are continually evolving, improving, and aligning with the needs and expectations of your students and the broader education community. This practice embodies the principles of the HAIL model, ensuring that your use of AI in education remains human-centered, adaptable, and consistently geared toward enhancing learning outcomes.

Encouraging Student Agency

Empowering students to play an active role in their learning, especially in the context of AI integration, is fundamental to fostering a sense of agency and ownership. When students are involved in selecting, evaluating, and even suggesting improvements for AI tools, they become more than just passive recipients of education; they become active participants in shaping their learning experiences. Here are some ways to encourage student agency in the context of AI integration in education.

Introduce students to a variety of AI tools and resources that could potentially be used in your lessons. Give them a basic overview of what each tool does and how it could enhance their learning. Organize sessions where students can experiment with these tools. Following these sessions, hold discussions or conduct surveys to gather their opinions on which tools they found most helpful or engaging.

Besides developing a systematic way for students to provide feedback on AI tools used in the classroom—and ensuring that they know their feedback is valued and will be seriously considered—you might assign students to evaluate specific features of an AI tool and present their findings to the class. This could involve researching the tool's efficacy, comparing it with other tools, or proposing ways it could be better integrated into the learning process. These evaluations not only encourage deeper engagement with the tool but also help students develop critical thinking and research skills.

Actively incorporate student feedback and suggestions into your lesson planning. For instance, if students express a preference for certain types of AI-driven activities, try to include these in your future lessons. Let students know how their feedback has shaped the lesson plan. This transparency reinforces the value of their input and further encourages active participation. You might collaborate with students on how best to integrate AI tools into their learning, such as by co-creating guidelines for tool usage, setting goals for AI-enhanced learning activities, or jointly developing criteria for evaluating the success of these activities.

Such collaboration not only boosts student engagement but also aligns AI usage more closely with their learning needs and preferences. It helps create an environment in which students feel comfortable experimenting with AI tools and suggesting innovative ways to use them. Encourage a mindset where trial and error are part of the learning process. Recognize and celebrate creative uses of AI tools by students. This recognition can motivate others to explore and suggest new ways of using these technologies.

By encouraging student agency in the selection, evaluation, and usage of AI tools, you empower your students and enrich the learning environment. This approach aligns with the HAIL model's emphasis on humanizing the education experience, ensuring that AI integration is guided by the needs, preferences, and creativity of the students themselves.

Conclusion: Embrace the Ongoing Process!

As we conclude this book, it's important to recognize that integrating AI into education is an ongoing process that evolves alongside technological and pedagogical advancements. This final section marks not an end but the start of a lasting pursuit of innovation and teaching excellence. The ever-changing nature of AI in education reflects this process—one filled with exploration, experimentation, and continuous learning.

The insights and strategies in this book are practical tools you can use and adapt in your daily teaching. They will help you create a lively, responsive, and continually improving classroom. Apply these strategies to fit your specific teaching context and meet your students' diverse needs. The main goal is to use AI to enhance—not replace—the human elements of teaching and learning, making education richer and more effective.

In this context, the work of Udvaros and Forman (2023) becomes particularly salient. They envision an Education 4.0 paradigm, one that embraces the principles of learning by doing, where AI and machine learning foster a constructive relationship between learners and educators. This paradigm shift is geared toward the individualized journey—where AI tools not only benefit personalized learning and development but also synergize with teachers to ensure optimal results. With AI integrated into teaching, the relationship between learners and educators becomes more collaborative and supportive. AI can handle routine tasks, such as grading and providing initial feedback, allowing educators to focus more on mentoring and engaging with students on a deeper level. This constructive relationship means that educators can use AI-generated insights to tailor their instruction to meet the unique needs of each student, fostering a more responsive and adaptive learning environment.

AI's ability to provide real-time data and analytics helps educators identify students' strengths and areas for improvement more effectively, enabling timely interventions and support. This hands-on learning experience through AI encourages a deeper, more confident mastery of skills that students can readily apply in real-life scenarios, moving away from the traditional, theoretical approach to a more practical, experiential learning process.

As you explore the potential of AI in education, consider the insights of Udvaros and Forman (2023). Embracing new technologies thoughtfully and optimistically can help us address current challenges and transform teaching and learning. AI is not just necessary; it is a guiding light toward a future of personalized, engaging, and empowering education. Remember, AI is a tool to enhance teaching—not replace it.

Your dedication to continuous improvement in integrating AI into your teaching will greatly influence your students' learning experiences. This commitment will shape how they perceive technology, engage with educational content, and develop academically. By incorporating AI, you will enhance their understanding and make learning more interactive and personalized.

Furthermore, your journey with AI will also shape your professional growth. As you integrate AI tools into your classroom, you will face new challenges that will push you to innovate and adapt. This process will not only benefit your students but also help you develop new skills and strategies, leading to professional development and success.

In summary, by committing to continuous improvement and embracing AI in your teaching, you will create a dynamic and enriching educational experience. This will positively influence your students' academic journeys and propel your own career forward as an educator who effectively utilizes technology.

Hold On to the HAIL Model

As you continue to integrate AI into your teaching, keep the HAIL model at the forefront. This framework has been your guide, balancing the integration of AI with a human-centered approach to education. It embodies the belief that the future of education depends on the collaboration between human touch and technological innovation, rather than their separation.

Now, as an educator, you're equipped to navigate the ever-changing landscape of AI in education. The HAIL model offers a clear direction: to create teaching methods that are not only effective but also empathetic, inclusive, and forward-thinking. Although this book has provided the foundation, the true application happens in your classroom. The future of education combines time-honored traditions with modern innovations, and you are the one shaping it. With AI as a tool and the HAIL model as your guide, you are ready to create an education experience that is as dynamic and diverse as your students.

Go Forth and Lead the Way

Approach the integration of AI in education with an open mind and a dedication to continuous learning. The potential of AI in education is vast and exciting. As you navigate this evolving landscape, remember that you are at the forefront of a major transformation in instruction. You have the power to shape not only the future of your students but also the direction of education itself. With the foundation laid in these chapters, you are well equipped to take on this challenge. So go forward, innovate, inspire, and lead the way in harnessing AI to create a more effective and equitable education system.

Always keep in mind that AI is a tool, not a replacement for the teacher. This principle should guide you as you continue to explore the possibilities of AI in education. Thoughtful integration of new technologies requires careful consideration of how they can support your goals, particularly in fostering creativity, curiosity, and collaboration among learners. Ensure that AI enhances the learning process rather than limits it. Focus on empowering students to take control of their learning, set their own goals, and engage deeply with the material.

This shift from traditional, closed-ended instructional methods to more open-ended, project-based learning can help students develop critical thinking, problem solving, and collaboration skills. AI has the potential to revolutionize education by making it more personalized and interactive. However, it is crucial to ensure that these technologies do not undermine the human connections that are essential to effective teaching. AI should be viewed as a valuable resource that supports teachers in their roles, providing them with tools to enhance their students' learning experiences.

The classroom should combine the best human qualities of teaching with the advanced capabilities of AI to create a more engaging and effective learning environment. The empathy, intuition, and personal connection that teachers bring to the classroom are irreplaceable and form the foundation of a nurturing educational experience. These human qualities foster a sense of community, support emotional well-being, and inspire students to explore and take risks in their learning. On the other hand, AI offers powerful tools that can enhance and complement these human elements. AI can provide personalized learning pathways, adapt to the individual needs of each student, and offer immediate feedback, thus allowing teachers to focus more on meaningful interactions and less on administrative tasks. By analyzing student data, AI can help identify areas where students are struggling and suggest targeted interventions, ensuring that no student is left behind.

Together, the human touch and AI's capabilities can transform the classroom into a dynamic and inclusive space. Teachers can use AI to introduce innovative teaching methods, create interactive and immersive learning experiences, and make informed decisions about curriculum design and instructional strategies. This synergy can lead to a more engaging environment in which students are motivated, supported, and empowered to achieve their full potential. In essence, the integration of AI in the classroom is not about replacing teachers but about augmenting their ability to connect with and inspire their students. By leveraging the strengths of both human educators and AI technologies, we can create a future where education is personalized, equitable, and profoundly impactful.

References

Adıgüzel, T., Kaya, M. H., & Cansu, F. K. (2023). Revolutionizing education with AI: Exploring the transformative potential of ChatGPT. *Contemporary Educational Technology, 15*(3).

Alasadi, E. A., & Baiz, C. R. (2023). Generative AI in education and research: Opportunities, concerns, and solutions. *Journal of Chemical Education, 100*(8), 2965–2971.

García-Peñalvo, F. J. (2023). The perception of artificial intelligence in educational contexts after the launch of ChatGPT: Disruption or panic? *Education in the Knowledge Society*, 24.

Holmes, W., & Tuomi, I. (2022). State of the art and practice in AI in education. *European Journal of Education, 57*(4), 542–570.

Mollick, E. (2024). Latent expertise: Everyone is in R&D. https://www.oneusefulthing.org/p/latent-expertise-everyone-is-in-r

Nguyen, N. D. (2023). Exploring the role of AI in education. *London Journal of Social Sciences*, (6), 84–95.

Puentedura, R. R. (2013, May 29). SAMR: Moving from enhancement to transformation. http://www.hippasus.com/rrpweblog/archives/000095.html

Schroeder, K. T., Hubertz, M., Van Campenhout, R., & Johnson, B. G. (2022). Teaching and learning with AI-generated courseware: Lessons from the classroom. *Online Learning, 26*(3), 73–87.

Udvaros, J., & Forman, N. (2023). Artificial intelligence and education 4.0. In *INTED2023 proceedings: 17th International Technology, Education and Development Conference* (pp. 6309–6317). IATED.

Index

The letter *f* following a page locator denotes a figure.

About the Author

Nathan D. Lang-Raad, EdD, is an educator, speaker, and author, as well as the founder and CEO of Raad Education, where he spearheads innovations in educational practice and theory.

Nathan's distinguished career encompasses roles as a teacher, an elementary and high school administrator, and a university adjunct professor. Notably, he has served as the director of elementary curriculum and instruction for Metropolitan Nashville Public Schools and as an education supervisor at NASA's Johnson Space Center. His previous positions include chief education officer at WeVideo and vice president of national product line at Savvas Learning.

A dedicated advocate for global sustainability, Nathan serves as the U.S. State Ambassador for the Climate Action Project, a collaborative initiative supported by the United Nations, World Wildlife Fund, NASA, and Jane Goodall Institute. He is also an advisor for Take Action Global (TAG).

An accomplished author, Nathan has contributed significantly to the education landscape, writing extensively about instructional coaching, innovative teaching methods, and the integration of technology in classrooms. His publications include *Everyday Instructional Coaching: Seven Daily Drivers to Support Teacher Effectiveness*; *The New Art and Science of Teaching Mathematics* (coauthored with Robert J. Marzano); *WeVideo Every Day: 40 Strategies to Deepen Learning in Any Class*; *Mathematics Unit Planning in a PLC at Work®, Grades PreK–2* (coauthored with Sarah Schuhl, Timothy D. Kanold, Jennifer Deinhart, Matthew R. Larson, and Nanci N. Smith); *The Teachers of Oz: Leading With Wisdom, Heart, Courage, and Spirit* (coauthored with Herbie Raad); *The Boundless Classroom: Designing Purposeful Instruction for Any Learning Environment* (coauthored with James Vince Witty); *Instructional Coaching Connection: Building Relationships to Better Support Teachers*; and *Never Stop Asking: Teaching Students to Be Better Critical Thinkers.*

Nathan earned a bachelor's degree in general science–chemistry from Harding University, a master's degree in administration and supervision from the University of Houston-Victoria, and a doctorate in learning organizations and strategic change from David Lipscomb University.

To learn more about Nathan's pioneering work, follow @drlangraad on X (formerly Twitter).

About ASCD Books

ASCD empowers educators to achieve excellence in learning, teaching, and leading so that each child is healthy, safe, engaged, supported, and challenged. Our books and quick reference guides feature a diversity of seasoned educators and new voices from all areas of the education community on both time-honored and timely topics like classroom management, instructional strategies, leadership, equity, and social-emotional learning. Our publications allow educators to chart their own learning journey so that they and their students can grow and flourish.

About ISTE Books

The International Society for Technology in Education (ISTE) is the leading publisher of books focused on technology in education. Our books and jump start guides promote revolutionary ideas and leading-edge practices that empower learning and teaching in a connected world. They cover a range of edtech topics and tie effective teaching and leadership strategies directly to the ISTE Standards, providing clear, practical guidance to help educators meet the Standards.

Related ISTE+ASCD Resources: Artificial Intelligence

At the time of publication, the following resources were available (ASCD stock numbers in parentheses).

AI for School Leaders: 62 Ways to Lighten Your Workload and Focus on What Matters by Vickie F. Echols

AI in the Classroom: Strategies and Activities to Enrich Student Learning (Jump Start Guide) by Nancye Blair Black

EdTech Essentials: 12 Strategies for Every Classroom in the Age of AI, 2nd Edition by Monica Burns (#124028)

How to Teach AI: Weaving Strategies and Activities Into Any Content Area by Rachelle Dené Poth

Principles and Practices for Effective Blended Learning (Quick Reference Guide) by Kristina Doubet and Eric M. Carbaugh (#QRG121056)

Summarization in Any Subject: 60 Innovative, Tech-Infused Strategies for Deeper Student Learning, 2nd Edition by Rick Wormeli and Dedra Stafford (#118048)

Tasks Before Apps: Designing Rigorous Learning in a Tech-Rich Classroom by Monica Burns (#118019)

Using AI Chatbots to Enhance Planning and Instruction (Quick Reference Guide) by Monica Burns (#QRG123066)

Using Technology in a Differentiated Classroom: Strategies and Tools for Designing Engaging, Effective, Efficient, and Equitable Learning by Clare Kilbane and Natalie Milman (#120002)

For up-to-date information about ASCD resources, go to www.ascd.org. You can search the complete archives of *Educational Leadership* at www.ascd.org/el.

For up-to-date information about ISTE resources, go to https://iste.org.

For more information, send an email to member@ascd.org; call 1-800-933-2723 or 703-578-9600; send a fax to 703-575-5400; or write to Information Services, ASCD, 2800 Shirlington Road, Suite 1001, Arlington, Virginia USA.

ascd whole child

The ASCD Whole Child approach is an effort to transition from a focus on narrowly defined academic achievement to one that promotes the long-term development and success of all children. Through this approach, ASCD supports educators, families, community members, and policymakers as they move from a vision about educating the whole child to sustainable, collaborative actions.

The AI Assist relates to the **engaged**, **supported**, and **challenged** tenets.
For more about the ASCD Whole Child approach, visit ***www.ascd.org/wholechild.***

WHOLE CHILD **TENETS**

1 **HEALTHY**
Each student enters school healthy and learns about and practices a healthy lifestyle.

2 **SAFE**
Each student learns in an environment that is physically and emotionally safe for students and adults.

3 **ENGAGED**
Each student is actively engaged in learning and is connected to the school and broader community.

4 **SUPPORTED**
Each student has access to personalized learning and is supported by qualified, caring adults.

5 **CHALLENGED**
Each student is challenged academically and prepared for success in college or further study and for employment and participation in a global environment.

Become an ASCD member today!
Go to www.ascd.org/joinascd
or call toll-free: 800-933-ASCD (2723)

DON'T MISS A SINGLE ISSUE OF ASCD'S AWARD-WINNING MAGAZINE.

ascd educational leadership

If you belong to a Professional Learning Community, you may be looking for a way to get your fellow educators' minds around a complex topic. Why not delve into a relevant theme issue of *Educational Leadership*, the journal written by educators for educators?

Subscribe now, or purchase back issues of ASCD's flagship publication at **www.ascd.org/el**. Discounts on bulk purchases are available.

To see more details about these and other popular issues of *Educational Leadership*, visit **www.ascd.org/el/all**.

2800 Shirlington Road
Suite 1001
Arlington, VA 22206 USA

www.ascd.org/learnmore